QUESTIONS & ANSWERS:
Environmental Law

Multiple Choice and Short Answer
Questions and Answers

By

DRU STEVENSON
Associate Professor of Law
South Texas College of Law

ISBN#: 1422406407

Editorial Offices
744 Broad Street, Newark, NJ 07102 (973) 820-2000
201 Mission St., San Francisco, CA 94105-1831 (415) 908-3200
701 East Water Street, Charlottesville, VA 22902-7587 (804) 972-7600
www.lexis.com

(Pub. 3232)

ABOUT THE AUTHOR

Dru Stevenson is an Associate Professor of Law at South Texas College of Law in Houston, where he teaches Environmental Law, Administrative Law, Economic Analysis of Law, and Criminal Law. Prior to entering the academy, Professor Stevenson served as an Assistant Attorney General for the State of Connecticut, in the Environmental Enforcement Division.

PREFACE

Environmental Law encompasses a host of federal and state statutes, common-law tort remedies, and a seemingly overwhelming body of administrative agency regulations. The policy issues involved in using laws to protect the environment involve (sometimes tragic) tradeoffs between economic growth, human health, and allocation of government resources in monitoring and enforcing compliance with the legal regime.

Most, if not all, law schools now offer courses in Environmental Law, ranging from an introductory survey course to upper-level electives and seminars devoted to specific topics, such as Water Law, Land Use, International Environmental Law, Animal Law, etc. Even students who do not intend to become practitioners specializing in Environmental Law often find these courses relevant to other intended career paths, such as Corporate Law, Real Estate practice, Energy Law, and Toxic Tort Litigation.

The purpose of this book is to test students' understanding of the areas most commonly included in an introductory or survey course of Environmental Law. Of course, every professor teaches this course somewhat differently, giving more emphasis to certain aspects than others. For example, some professors give little or no attention to Administrative Law or the Common Law in their Environmental Law courses, as these subjects have entire courses devoted to them at most law schools. Others feel that these subjects are controlling of much of the court decisions in Environmental Law, and therefore address them at considerable length in their courses. Similarly, courses vary in how much emphasis they give to background policy issues like cost-benefit analysis and the problem of scientific uncertainty and risk management. This book attempts to give some treatment to these subjects, but students should focus most of the subjects included in their own course syllabus. Absent from this book is the Endangered Species Act, which most introductory courses (and casebooks) in Environmental Law tend to omit.

This book is not intended to provide a definitive or complete explanation of Environmental regulations. Instead, it is a supplement to regular class materials, and opportunity for students to test their knowledge in preparation for a final exam. I also generally avoided tangential issues like constitutional "Takings" jurisprudence, municipal zoning, and international law — again, because I believe many Environmental Law survey courses do not reach these matters, leaving them instead for advanced-level electives and seminar courses.

Dru Stevenson
Houston, Texas
February 2007

TABLE OF CONTENTS

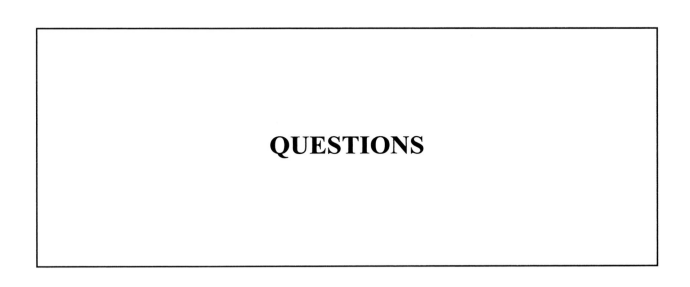

QUESTIONS

Constitutional Limits. This section covers basic constitutional issues included in many Environmental Law casebooks: issues of Federal vs. State Regulation, Federal Pre-emption of State Statutes, "Dormant Commerce Clause Power," and the Nondelegation Doctrine.

1. Despite Constitutional concerns about states' rights to regulate their own environment, the most common policy argument in favor of federal regulation of the environment is:

    (A) It is always better to have all the power consolidated in a few individuals.

    (B) Air and water pollution migrate across state lines every day, creating chronic practical problems regarding venue and jurisdiction for those seeking legal redress.

    (C) The Privilege and Immunities Clause of the Fourteenth Amendment.

    (D) The need for states to collaborate in their efforts to clean up the environment.

2. The "nondelegation doctrine" in Supreme Court jurisprudence limits the government's ability to:

    (A) Regulate areas previously dominated by common law.

    (B) Entrust enforcement powers to the Executive Branch.

    (C) Entrust rulemaking and adjudicatory powers to administrative agencies.

    (D) Regulate areas traditionally governed individually by the states.

3. To escape invalidation by the courts under the nondelegation doctrine, an environmental statute must include:

    (A) Detailed and comprehensive provisions about the scope of authority or powers being delegated.

    (B) A clear statement of the Congressional intent or purpose behind the statute and the regulations that depend on it.

    (C) Provisions pertaining to the appointment and removal powers of the agency leadership.

    (D) Intelligible standards that give some guidance about what Congress intends.

4. The "nondelegation doctrine" is based primarily on:

    (A) The Separation of Powers as expressed in the "vesting clauses" of the Constitution.

    (B) The Nondelegation Clause.

    (C) The Tenth Amendment.

    (D) The Commerce Clause.

5. Describe briefly the relationship between federalism and the common law rules about protecting the environment.

ANSWER:

6. Johnny Appleseed hears that loggers are chopping down thousands of wild apple trees in other states. He is terribly upset by this news, even though he has never visited these states, and immediately brings an action in federal court to enjoin this destruction of the environment. What is the first legal obstacle his case will encounter?

    (A) The loggers have already obtained a permit from the relevant regulatory agencies to carry on this activity.

    (B) The value of the wood from these apple trees, and the value of developing the previously-undeveloped woodlands, far outweighs the loss of a few wild apple trees.

    (C) Appleseed lacks standing to bring the action.

    (D) Appleseed has no evidence to support his claims, as he has not even seen the trees in question or visited these states.

7. What are the traditional elements to determine if a plaintiff has "standing" to bring an action in court?

    (A) Likelihood of prevailing on the merits, irreparable harm if the court does not intervene immediately, and "clean hands," i.e., the plaintiff did not contribute to the harm.

    (B) Legitimate government interest in addressing the harm involved, and a remedy narrowly tailored to achieve this public purpose.

    (C) Statutory authorization to bring this type of action instead of the relevant enforcement agency.

    (D) Injury in fact, causation, and redressability of harm.

8. The State of New York decides the EPA's regulation of air pollution has not worked well, and decides to create its own body of state law to limit emissions of air pollutants and balance the competing interests of the state economy (i.e., industry) and the state environment. The state legislature creates a body of law that contradicts federal regulations on several points. When the regulated industry contests these new rules in court, what is the likely result?

    (A) The court will invalidate New York's regulations under the Supremacy Clause of the U.S. Constitution.

    (B) The court will invalidate the state regulations under the Commerce Clause of the U.S. Constitution.

    (C) The court will invalidate the state regulations under the "Dormant Commerce Clause Power" of Congress.

    (D) The court will uphold the state statute.

9. The State of Ohio passes a regulation prohibiting the importation of trash from another state, citing the problem of Ohio landfills overflowing with trash from Illinois and Indiana. How are the courts likely to analyze the constitutionality of this regulation?

    (A) The court will invalidate New York's regulations under the Supremacy Clause of the U.S. Constitution.

    (B) The court will invalidate the state regulations under the Nondelegation Clause of the U.S. Constitution.

    (C) The court will invalidate the state regulations under the "Dormant Commerce Clause Power" of Congress.

    (D) The court will ask the EPA to review the state statute.

10. Which jurisprudential doctrine below reflects judicial suspicion of administrative agencies like the EPA?

    (A) *Chevron* Doctrine.

    (B) Dormant Commerce Clause Power.

    (C) Nondelegation Doctrine.

    (D) Federal Pre-emption.

11. Amy is alarmed at the deterioration of the environment that she observes around her, and even more concerned about cataclysmic climate changes that might result from human-produced greenhouse gases. She concludes that the existing statutory framework is inadequate to safeguard against environmental catastrophe. In an attempt to force

change, she files suit against the President, the EPA, and Congress itself, claiming that her constitutional right to a clean environment must be upheld. Is there a constitutional right to a clean environment? Why or why not?

ANSWER:

Administrative Regulation. This section addresses basic issues of Notice-and-Comment Rulemaking, "Scope of Authority" under Agency Enabling Statutes, Rulemaking vs. Adjudication, Licensing and Reporting Requirements, Negotiated Rulemaking, Agency Capture, Executive Control over EPA policy and directors, Congressional Control over EPA's authority and mandates, Agency interpretation of statutes, requirements and prohibitions of cost-benefit analysis in regulatory actions, and prosecutorial discretion.

12. The Sierra Club is litigating under the APA to contest the Atomic Agency's newly-promulgated rule about nuclear power plants. While admitting that the agency followed the required notice-and-comment procedures, the Sierra Club argues that there was no opportunity to cross-examine high-ranking agency officials in a public hearing. The Club contends that the lack of a fair hearing deprived its members of their due process rights. How is a court likely to respond to this argument?

    (A) A court will probably find there is no APA hearing requirement because this is rulemaking instead of adjudication.

    (B) A court will probably use "remand without vacatur" and require the agency to hold some hearings before implementing its final rule.

    (C) A court will probably find that the lack of a public hearing was itself a violation of the APA's notice-and-comment requirements.

    (D) A court will probably find that there is no hearing requirement because the APA specifically exempts agency actions related to national security or nuclear power.

13. Charged by Congress with the job of limiting carbon dioxide emissions, the EPA decides to create a program issuing permits and licenses for emitters, instead of issuing a ban or prohibition. Which of the following is not a reason the EPA would be issuing permits to pollute?

    (A) The permit applications usually contain extensive reporting requirements, which provide the EPA with useful data about the true sources and quantity of emissions.

    (B) The permit applications encourage voluntary reductions in pollution because the polluters must disclose what they are doing.

(C)   The permit program allows the President to get around Congressional intent, allowing emissions instead of reducing them.

(D)   The permit system allows the EPA to attach conditions for renewal of permits later, once the holder of the permit has made substantial investments in developing the business.

14.   Dump-n-run Corp. holds a permit for discharging small quantities of non-toxic waste into the river that runs alongside its production facility. After several complaints about this company's pollution, and a series of acrimonious conversations with the permit-issuing agency, the agency refuses to renew the permit the following year. Dump-n-run challenges the loss of its permit in court, claiming that the agency failed to follow APA notice-and-comment requirements before making its final decision about this permit. How will the court react to this argument?

(A)   The court will invalidate the agency's action and reinstate the permit, due to the APA violation.

(B)   The court will probably find that the agency's action violated the Due Process Clause of the Constitution because Dump-n-Run did not have a hearing before the permit expired.

(C)   The court will probably find that that the APA's requirements do not apply here, because this is informal rulemaking instead of formal rulemaking.

(D)   The court will probably find the APA's requirements do not apply here, because this is informal adjudication instead of rulemaking.

15.   The EPA adopts an internal policy that it will bring enforcement actions only against large corporate polluters that have more than $50 million in revenue every year, as part of the President's overall policy of protecting small business owners. One of the large corporate defendants challenges this policy through litigation, claiming that is discriminates against larger companies, that it creates inequalities and unfairness, and violates substantive due process under the Fourteenth Amendment of the Constitution. How will these arguments stand up in court?

(A)   The court will probably defer to the agency's discretion in deciding which violators to prosecute.

(B)   The court will probably find that the EPA has gone outside its statutory authority.

(C)   The court will probably find that the EPA violated the APA's notice-and-comment rules if this new policy was not first published in the Federal Register.

(D)   The court will probably look at the legislative history of the relevant statute to see if the EPA should have this level of discretion.

16. Sometimes the EPA invites representatives from the regulated industry to meet and discuss the best means to reduce a certain type of pollution. When the parties disagree, the EPA continues to negotiate until everyone reaches a compromise and there is consensus. Then, instead of publishing a rule in the Federal Register, the EPA uses quasi-contractual consent agreements by which each party pledges to uphold their end of the agreement. The EPA thus avoids the long, tedious procedure of promulgating rules, litigating over the validity of the rules, and trying to enforce the rules uniformly. How do we usually describe this scenario in environmental law?

   (A) "Agency Capture."

   (B) "Collective Bargaining."

   (C) "Command-and-control Rulemaking" or "C.A.C. Rulemaking."

   (D) "Reg-neg" or "Negotiated Rulemaking."

17. Which of the following is NOT one of the ways that Congress controls the EPA?

   (A) Congress votes on the EPA's budget each year.

   (B) Congress can remove the Administrator of the EPA at will.

   (C) Congress enacts and can amend the agency's enabling statute.

   (D) Congress can negate specific regulations through subsequent regulation.

18. Suppose an environmental statute gives the Administrator full discretion to promulgate rules to "prevent any harm to rabbits." The EPA interprets this phrase to include indirect harms, such as the elimination of natural predators on rabbits (like wolves), because fewer natural predators will cause rabbits to multiply too rapidly, leading eventually to an overpopulation of rabbits and starvation if the rabbits in a given area cannot expand their food supply. A real estate developer finds its project stymied because it could kill a few wolves — but under the pretext of the EPA's rabbit-protecting authority. The developer contests the action in court, claiming that the statutory authorizes the EPA to protect rabbits, and protecting rabbits' natural predators would seem to do the exact opposite. What is the likely result in court?

   (A) The court will probably defer to the agency's interpretation of an ambiguous provision in the statute.

   (B) The court will find that the agency exceeded its statutory authority.

   (C) The court will find that the agency violated an essential provision of the APA.

   (D) The court will find that the agency's action runs afoul of the Nondelegation Doctrine.

19. Suppose Congress creates a new agency to stop global warming and regulate carbon dioxide emissions, especially from vehicles. To direct this new agency, the President appoints Leigh Imacuckoo, the former CEO of a major automobile manufacturer. Mr. Imacuckoo has undisputed expertise in vehicle emissions, the economic feasibility of different alternatives for controlling vehicle emissions, and the projected number of vehicles that will be on the roads for the next several years. The new Director immediately promulgates a body of regulations that are very favorable to the automobile industry, and which do very little to reduce emissions. What do we call this (rather commonplace) scenario?

   (A) "Ultra vires."

   (B) "Regulation running riot."

   (C) "Agency Capture."

   (D) "Failed states."

20. What is the main way that the President of the United States controls the Environmental Protection Agency?

   (A) The President controls its budget and the salaries of its workers.

   (B) The President appoints the Administrator (who heads the EPA) and regional directors.

   (C) The President is the Commander-in-Chief of the agency and can simply order it to do what the President wants.

   (D) The President decides what regulations the agency will promulgate.

21. Suppose the President wants to force the EPA to consider the overall economic costs of proposed regulations, even where Congress did not require this. What is the most effective legal tool in achieving this goal?

   (A) Certain provisions of the Administrative Procedure Act that require agencies to be "reasonable."

   (B) The President can threaten to fire the EPA Administrator.

   (C) The President can require the EPA to include economic considerations in its Environmental Impact Statement under certain provisions of NEPA.

   (D) The President can require the EPA to submit a cost-benefit analysis of the proposed regulation to the Office of Management and Budget before publishing it in the Federal Register.

22. Suppose Congress passes a new statute called the Clean Dirt Act, authorizing the EPA to "take whatever actions are necessary to preserve and maintain the health and cleanliness of our precious loam." The EPA is much more concerned about the threat of bioterrorism and home-made bombs, so it exercises its authority under the act to restrict sales of fertilizers, like those used in the Oklahoma City bombing. The EPA attaches some regulatory rhetoric about this being necessary to protect the soils from fertilizers. When the fertilizer industry challenges the regulations in court, what would be their strongest legal argument, based on these facts?

    (A) The agency exceeded its statutory authority.

    (B) The agency violated the U.S. Constitution.

    (C) The agency failed to follow the APA.

    (D) The agency misinterpreted the statute.

23. The EPA decides to generate some goodwill in the community by allowing local church groups to meet in their regional office conference rooms and lunchrooms on the weekends. A local Objectivist Society requests the use of a meeting room, and the EPA denies the request, as retaliation for an anti-environmentalist symposium the group sponsored the previous year. Furious, the Objectivist Society files a lawsuit, claiming viewpoint discrimination, Establishment Clause violations, and so on. What legal argument from Administrative Law might help the Society challenge the EPA's actions?

    (A) The agency did not have a Notice-and-Comment period about its decision to deny access to the Objectivist Society.

    (B) The agency exceeded its statutory authority in allowing anyone to use its facilities on weekends.

    (C) The agency failed to provide a fair hearing to the Society before denying them access to the meeting rooms.

    (D) The agency failed to articulate a reasonable basis for its decision.

24. Esther is a regional director for the EPA, and she decides to focus her region's enforcement activities on the very worst polluters (in terms of quantity), rather than spreading the agency's resources too thinly across cases of lesser significance. The National Resource Defense Council (NRDC) sues the agency to compel uniform enforcement against all violators; and the defendants in Esther's cases, the major polluters, raise a defense of due process violations for the disparate treatment received

by different violators of the same statute. What will be the likely response to these arguments by the courts?

ANSWER:

25. Hal has operated his car washing business for some time, under the appropriate permits. Recently, however, the state environmental enforcement agency received notice that he is performing oil changes and radiator flushes for some cars, and that he allows the old oil and radiator fluid to drain into the nearby ditch as well. The agency now revokes his discharge permit, which jeopardizes his business. What is Hal's first line of legal recourse?

    (A) He can sue the agency for an unconstitutional "taking."

    (B) He can probably request an administrative hearing where he can rebut the allegations.

    (C) He can sue the agency for unconstitutional interference with his contract rights.

    (D) He has no recourse whatsoever.

26. The EPA decides to promulgate a new rule governing carbon dioxide emission from automobiles. They hold a press conference announcing that henceforth, carbon dioxide emissions from cars will have to meet certain requirements. The regulations appear in the next edition of the Code of Federal Regulations, and the agency commences enforcement actions. Given these facts, what error did the agency make in its procedure?

    (A) The agency failed to seek the permission of Congress before regulating this area.

    (B) The agency failed to comply with the APA's Notice-and-Comment requirements.

    (C) The agency failed to operate within its statutory authority.

    (D) There is no error; the agency followed proper protocol.

27. Which is most true of the Administrative Procedure Act (APA) as is applies to environmental agencies?

    (A) The APA requires agencies to consider the costs or burdens of regulations before promulgating any new rules.

    (B) The APA requires agencies to have public hearings on any matter that the regulated industry wants to dispute.

    (C)   The APA requires agencies to get court approval before engaging in agency adjudications.

    (D)   The APA requires agencies to publish proposed rules in the Federal Register and allow a reasonable time for comments from the public before issuing a final rule.

28.   What type of action does the APA not contemplate for governmental agencies?

    (A)   Interpreting the Constitution.

    (B)   Quasi-legislative rulemaking.

    (C)   Quasi-judicial adjudication.

    (D)   Issuing permits and licenses.

29.   Suppose the National Fish & Wildlife Service decides to list several species of slugs as "endangered" under the Endangered Species Act, and publishes its intended listing in the Federal Register. During the comment period, several environmentalist groups submit comments challenging the inclusion of certain bats and the omission of others from the list. In its Notice of Final Rule, the agency publishes a completely different list, based on the comments it received from the public. When affected industries challenge the rule, what will be the result in court?

    (A)   A court will uphold the rule because it complied with the Notice-and-Comment requirements of the APA.

    (B)   A court will invalidate the rule because the agency should have published the rule in the Code of Federal Regulations instead.

    (C)   A court will invalidate the rule because the final rule is too different from the original rule, thus violating the APA's Notice-and-Comment requirements.

    (D)   A court will uphold the rule, because the agency has full discretion to list any species it wants as "endangered."

Judicial Review. This section covers the *Chevron* Doctrine, *Overton Park* standards for judicial review, standing for challenging agency actions, and the need for agencies to create a "record" of decision processes.

30.   What is the most common standard of review for administrative agency actions, which the Supreme Court articulated in the famous *Overton Park* case and its progeny?

    (A)   The Substantial Evidence test.

    (B)   The Reasonableness test.

    (C)   De Novo Review.

    (D)   Arbitrary & Capricious/Abuse of Discretion.

31. Larry feels he is the victim of overzealous enforcement by the EPA, and he brings a suit challenging a recent final decision from the agency that was adverse to his interests. Before reaching the merits of his claim, the court must consider the EPA's Motion to Dismiss, which asserts hat there is no statute explicitly giving Larry the right to judicial review for this particular action. How will the court probably respond?

    (A)   The EPA will lose on this motion because there is a presumption in favor of judicial review, unless Congress has statutorily barred review of this specific agency action.

    (B)   The EPA will prevail on its motion because there is a presumption against reviewability for agency actions in the absence of clear statutory authorization for judicial review.

    (C)   The EPA will lose on its motion because it lacks statutory authority to file such motions.

    (D)   The EPA will prevail because Larry's case is not yet ripe.

32. Which two clauses of the United States Constitution are most likely to furnish the basis for a challenge to administrative regulatory action?

    (A)   The Nondelegation clause and the Due Process clause.

    (B)   The Due Process clause and the Takings Clause.

    (C)   The Takings Clause and the Contracts Clause.

    (D)   The Equal Protection Clause and the Due Process Clause.

33. What are the three parts of the constitutional requirements for "standing," according to the Supreme Court?

    (A)   Injury-in-fact, causation, and redressibility.

    (B)   Injury-in-fact, ripeness, and mootness.

    (C)   Causation, redressibility, and jurisdiction.

    (D)   Injury-in-fact, domicile, and ripeness.

34. *Chevron*, the most-cited case of all time, was actually about:

    (A)   The Reagan-era EPA's "bubble theory."

    (B)   Estuaries.

    (C)   Oil and gas regulations.

    (D)   The nondelegation doctrine.

35. Suppose the EPA publishes a Notice of Intended Rulemaking in the Federal Register, stating that it plans to promulgate stringent new carbon dioxide emission standards for automobiles. It solicits public comments, and most of the comments come from environmentalist groups concerned about global warming caused by carbon dioxide emissions. The automobile industry maintains that it cannot possible reduce carbon dioxide emissions very far, given the current technology, and immediately brings suit to challenge the proposed rule, asserting due process concerns, various procedural defects in the publication, etc. What is the EPA's best argument for seeking dismissal of such actions?

   (A) The petitioners are not the parties being injured by carbon dioxide emissions, so they lack standing.

   (B) The agency is clearly acting within its statutory authority in making this rule.

   (C) The case is not yet ripe because there is no final decision by the agency.

   (D) The agency duly complied with all technical requirements of the APA.

36. What are the two prongs of the so-called "*Chevron* test"?

   (A) Whether the agency acted within its statutory authority, and whether the agency articulated the basis for its decision.

   (B) Whether the agency considered public comments and responded to the comments when it published its Final Rule in the Federal Register.

   (C) Whether Congress used ambiguous terms in the relevant statute, and whether the agency's interpretation of the ambiguous terms was reasonable.

   (D) Whether Congress' intent is clear in the statute, and whether the agency complied with Congress' intent.

37. Under the Administrative Procedures Act, courts generally apply the "substantial evidence" test to what kind of actions by environmental agencies?

   (A) Formal, on-the-record rulemaking.

   (B) Informal rulemaking.

   (C) Informal adjudication.

   (D) Internal agency decisions about how to conduct rulemaking.

38. Darrow Corp. receives an Administrative Order from the EPA demanding that it participate in a "removal" cleanup action under CERCLA. Darrow Corp. believes the EPA has committed several legal and factual errors in issuing this Order, and immediately brings suit in federal district court to have the Order rescinded. The EPA

contends that Section 113(h) of the CERCLA statute makes judicial review unavailable to Darrow Crop. What is the like outcome of this dispute?

(A) The court will recognize an absolute presumption in favor of judicial review of agency actions, for public policy reasons.

(B) The court will take a "hard look" at whether the agency articulated the reason for its decision, and then side with the agency if the reason is articulated in the record.

(C) The court will dismiss the case for lacking ripeness, as this is merely a pre-enforcement Administrative Order.

(D) The court will dismiss the case because Congress has made the decision "unreviewable" by courts.

39. Under the Administrative Procedures Act, courts generally apply the "arbitrary and capricious" standard to what kind of actions by environmental agencies?

(A) Formal, on-the-record rulemaking.

(B) Informal rulemaking.

(C) Informal adjudication.

(D) Internal agency decisions about how to conduct rulemaking.

40. The so-called *Chevron* test mandates judicial deference to what kind of agency action?

(A) Agency decisions about whether to use informal or formal rulemaking procedures.

(B) Agency interpretations of statutory language.

(C) Agency decisions about whether to use adjudication or rulemaking to further its policies.

(D) Agency rationalizations for decisions, as documented in the record.

41. Wilma and Betty live in Maine, but they are very concerned about the effects of U.S. Navy submarine exercises on dolphins in the Pacific Ocean. They are members of a club named Dolphins Are People, Too (DAPT). Neither of them has ever seen a dolphin or has ever left the state of Maine, but they bring suit under the Marine Mammal Protection Act (MMPA) to enjoin the Navy from harming the dolphins with their submarine exercise. Will they have standing to bring this suit as members of DAPT?

(A) Yes, if the MMPA has a citizen-suit provision allowing environmentalist groups like DAPT to intervene on behalf of the dolphins.

(B) No, because their lack of contact with the dolphins, or likelihood of future contact, means they have not suffered an injury-in-fact.

(C)   Yes, because Congress clearly intended to protect the dolphins when it enacted the MMPA.

(D)   No, because an organization or club does not have standing to represent the interests of individual members like Wilma and Betty.

42.   The "hard look" doctrine in refers to what type of judicial analysis?

(A)   De novo review of agency findings of fact.

(B)   The "substantial evidence" rule for agency findings of fact.

(C)   The "rational basis" test for agency decisions.

(D)   Strict scrutiny of whether the agency articulated the basis for its decision in the record.

43.   The so-called *Vermont Yankee* rule mandates judicial deference to what kind of agency action?

(A)   Agency decisions about whether to use informal or formal rulemaking procedures.

(B)   Agency interpretations of statutory language.

(C)   Agency decisions about whether to use adjudication or rulemaking to further its policies.

(D)   Agency rationalizations for decisions, as documented in the record.

44.   When a court decides to evaluate an EPA action to determine if the action was "arbitrary and capricious" or an "abuse of discretion," what will the court require from the agency?

(A)   Technical adherence to the APA's Notice-and-Comment requirements.

(B)   Whether "reasonable minds could differ" about the correctness of the agency's decision.

(C)   "Substantial evidence" in the record that supports the agency's position.

(D)   A clear articulation of the basis for the agency's decision.

45.   Clarence needs to challenge an agency action on behalf of his client, whose water discharge permit was recently revoked. Not finding any provisions for judicial review in the relevant permitting statutes or regulation, on what basis can Clarence seek judicial review of the agency's action, besides bringing a constitutional due process claim?

(A)   The Administrative Review Act, Section 5.

(B)   The Administrative Procedure Act, Section 7.

(C)   NEPA.

(D)   FOIA.

46.   Which jurisprudential doctrine reflects judicial deference to administrative agencies like the EPA?

(A)   *Chevron* Doctrine.

(B)   Dormant Commerce Clause Power.

(C)   Nondelegation Doctrine.

(D)   Federal Pre-emption.

47. Senator Ulltrac Onservatiff laments the advent of federal environmental statutes. He longs for a return to the good old days, when courts regulated environmental harms through common law nuisance claims. He says that one-size-fits-all regulations are economically burdensome, insensitive to local and regional differences, and ineffectual because of the political compromises that dilute the final versions of most environmental statutes. Which of the following was a chronic problem with using common law nuisance to address environmental harms?

    (A) The states had engaged in a cut-throat "race-to-the-bottom" to attract heavy industry to their locale.

    (B) It simply cost too much to enforce.

    (C) The defendants had an incentive to kill their victims before they filed lawsuits.

    (D) The harms were often spread over such a diffuse area that no single plaintiff had sufficient incentive to bring the action, or lacked sufficient particularized harm to prevail.

48. Professor Frankenstein is an independent biochemist who works under contracts with the Defense Department to do biological-warfare research in his private laboratory. All the wells in the area soon have contamination from sarin and cyanide, and many pets in the neighborhood have contracted Anthrax. A flurry of lawsuits ensues, claiming he should be liable. Frankenstein obtained the necessary permits and security clearance to purchase, produce, and experiment with sarin, cyanide, and anthrax; he can document that his laboratory complies with industry standards, and materials are handled and stored with due care and diligence. Under common law, can he escape liability by showing he was not negligent, or by showing he had a license or permit?

    (A) If he can defeat any allegations of negligence, he will escape liability, regardless of permits and licenses.

    (B) He will be liable regardless of negligence or permits, because engaging in ultra hazardous activities — even if completely legal and beneficial to society — carries strict liability.

    (C) If he has the necessary permits and licenses, he will escape liability regardless of the negligence issue.

(D)   Regardless of permits and licenses, Dr. Frankenstein was clearly negligent, *res ipsa loquitur*, because of the contamination in the neighborhood.

49.   Regardless of the theory of liability in the problem above, Dr. Frankenstein maintains that his laboratory and experiments did not cause the contamination of wells in the area or the diseases befalling the pets. He maintains that some wells had contamination before he moved to the area, and the contamination in the other wells predated his arrival but was only recently discovered. He similarly maintains that the pets are sick from a naturally-occurring outbreak of anthrax, probably originating at the sheep harm in the next county. How will this affect the outcome of the cases against him?

(A)   If the court uses a theory of strict liability, causation will be irrelevant.

(B)   If the court uses a *res ipsa loquitur* theory of negligence, causation will be irrelevant.

(C)   If the court uses a theory of strict liability, the plaintiffs must still prove causation, which is difficult with environmental harms like this.

(D)   If the court uses a theory of negligence, Dr. Frankenstein will have the burden of showing he did not cause these harms that seem to correlate with his activities.

50.   Which of the following was NOT a reason to move away from a common law system for addressing environmental harms?

(A)   Water and air pollution migrate such great distances that it becomes difficult to locate the appropriate defendant.

(B)   The harm to individual plaintiffs was often too small to offset the costs of bringing a lawsuit, even if the aggregate harm was enormous.

(C)   Common law judges were completely unsympathetic to nuisance plaintiffs, leaving most without real judicial recourse.

(D)   Pollution or contamination would migrate across state lines, creating jurisdictional problems and conflicts of laws.

51.   Aglow Industries processes the radioactive material contained in household smoke alarms. Aglow has a little accident at their plant four years ago, when some low-grade radioactive material fell into a deep well on their back lot. Soon all the wells in the area had elevated levels of radiation in them, but so far no one is sick. The city fixed the situation by running municipal water lines to all the homes and sealing all the wells, so there should be no future exposure to radiation from the wells. Knowing that the previous five years of radiation exposure could cause cancer, area resident bring a common law nuisance, strict liability, and negligence. What is the weakest part of their case?

(A)   They cannot allege nuisance and negligence at the same time, even as alternate theories.

(B)   They probably cannot prove causation, because so many things in our environment and lifestyles cause cancer.

(C)   The town has rendered the problem moot by supplying municipal water.

(D)   They cannot demonstrate any harm besides fear of getting cancer in the future, which courts treat skeptically.

52.   Assuming the facts above, suppose one plaintiff, Rip Van Winkle, has developed stomach cancer from the five years of exposure to radiation in his well. He brings a civil action immediately and wins, and then goes through chemotherapy and fully recovers from his stomach cancer. Twenty years later, every single person who drank water from the contaminated wells has colon cancer, including Rip, and experts demonstrate a clear link to Aglow's incident. Brimming with confidence because of his success in his previous lawsuit, Rip sues the tannery again for his new cancer. Will Rip have the same chances of success this time?

(A)   His chances of success are even better, because so many people have the same sickness from the same contamination.

(B)   His chances are much worse — a court will probably dismiss his new action, because the same plaintiff cannot bring multiple actions arising from the same set of facts.

(C)   His chances are worse, because the long period of time that has elapsed will make a court skeptical that the cancer was caused by Aglow industries.

(D)   His chances are better, because it is rare for the same person to get cancer twice, making his claim of exposure to carcinogenic radiation more credible.

53.   How has CERCLA impacted nuisance actions?

(A)   CERCLA has boosted them.

(B)   CERCLA has pre-empted them.

(C)   CERCLA has limited them.

(D)   CERCLA depends on them.

54.   The Sierra Club brings a private nuisance action against an old tannery in Woburn, MA, whose negligent practices have contaminated the wells in the area, and the underground water supply. The rear acreage of the Sierra Club's property abuts the old tannery, but its building sits facing Main Street in downtown Woburn, enabling the Sierra Club to connect to the city water system, which brings water from an uncontaminated spring

high in the Berkshire Mountains. What effect will the Sierra Club's enjoyment of city water have on its civil action for contamination of the wells in that area?

(A) It will have no effect, because nuisance actions can be based on purely aesthetic or prospective harms.

(B) It will probably defeat their claim, because the old tannery has not interfered with the Sierra Club's use and enjoyment of their property.

(C) It will bolster their claim, because the existence of a municipal water supply suggests there is some widespread problem with the wells.

(D) It will defeat their claim, because it enables the tannery to argue that it did not cause the contamination to the Sierra Club's property.

55.   The four main types of remedies available for environmental nuisance actions are:

(A) Before-and-after rule, special damages, punitive damages, and injunctions.

(B) Injunctions, executions, evictions, and terminations.

(C) Criminal liability, civil liability, and strict liability.

(D) Injunctions, money, promises, and handshakes.

56.   The State Attorney General brings a civil action for public nuisance against a private junkyard that shreds cars and sells the scrap metal, because for decades the junk cars of leaked PCB's into the soil and caused contamination of the a few wells in the neighborhood. The junkyard has violated some technical provisions of its state permits and licenses. What type of analysis is the court likely to use in determining liability, in this type of public nuisance action brought by a government official?

(A) A court will probably use a strict liability approach for a public nuisance action brought by the Attorney General, especially if there are some violations of administrative regulations.

(B) A court will probably use a cost-benefit approach to balance the utility of the defendant's conduct with the extent of the harm caused.

(C) A court will probably dismiss the action because it does not allege a harm that affects everyone in the state equally.

(D) A court will probably find that the Attorney General does not have standing to bring the action, because public nuisance actions should be brought by private plaintiffs.

57.   For better or worse, the federal common law of nuisance has been:

(A) Bolstered by statute.

(B)   Overused to the point of tedium.

(C)   Pre-empted by federal regulation where applicable.

(D)   Created "sua sponte" by the liberal Warren Court.

58.   Morgan does not want to pay for garbage removal, so he digs a big pit in his backyard and throws all his garbage in it, for several years. Before he sells his property, he covers the garbage pit with dirt and sod, rendering it invisible. He sells the property to Lawrence, who takes up residence there. Lawrence soon notices a foul stench in the backyard, which was not apparent on the day he inspected the property before his purchase, because it was a windy, blustery day. In addition, whenever it rains, the rainwater seeping into the nearby storm ditch is black and smells awful. His pets always seem to die after a few weeks, usually after minor digging in the dirt in the backyard. Lawrence eventually learns of Morgan's old garbage pit and sues him under the common law of property. What type of action would this be under property law?

(A)   Public nuisance.

(B)   Waste.

(C)   Interference with quiet enjoyment.

(D)   Adverse possession.

59.   Elmer Fudd is tired of his neighbor, who raises rabbits, allowing hundreds of crazed rabbits to run loose all over the neighborhood about once a month. The rabbits come onto Fudd's property and cause minor damage. Sometimes their owner enters the property to retrieve his rabbits. Fudd is trying to decide whether to bring an action for trespass or nuisance. His lawyer, Daffy, tells him that the choice depends in part on which type of common law property right is most at stake. What is the correct correlation of rights to actions below?

(A)   Nuisance protects exclusive possession and trespass protects quiet enjoyment.

(B)   Nuisance protects one's living quarters and trespass protects one's land.

(C)   Nuisance protects one from invasions, and trespass protects from intruders.

(D)   Trespass protects exclusive possession and nuisance protects quiet enjoyment.

60.   For Elmer Fudd, wanting to sue over the destructive invasion of his property by rabbits, what is one significant advantage of bringing an action in nuisance instead of trespass?

(A)   Trespass normally requires a showing of intent by the defendant, while nuisance may not require this.

(B)   Trespass has a shorter statute of limitations than nuisance.

(C)   Trespass forces the plaintiff to demonstrate ownership of the property invaded.

(D)   Trespass has been abolished by statute in most jurisdictions, whereas nuisance is alive and well.

61.   Attorney Daffy Duck advises his client, Fudd, that there are also come advantages to suing for trespass instead of nuisance. Which of the following is NOT an advantage of trespass over nuisance?

(A)   The statute of limitations for trespass often extends further back in time than it does for nuisance.

(B)   Trespass actions are more likely to obtain injunctions because they focus on invasions or intrusions against consent, rather than ongoing annoyances.

(C)   Trespass actions require a showing of intent, whereas nuisance actions require a showing of negligence, which is less tangible and more difficult to prove.

(D)   If there is a "direct" trespass, the plaintiff does not have to show substantial damages (unlike nuisance), and can obtain punitive damages based on a showing of nominal harm.

62.   When Elmer Fudd sues his neighbor under both trespass and nuisance for his repeated practice of turning thousands of crazed rabbits loose in the neighborhood, the neighbor raises the defense that Fudd's property value has increased as a result of the rabbits, because it is a desirable location for game hunters and scientists wanting to conduct pharmaceutical experiments on rabbits. The defendant submits as evidence an independent property appraisal confirming that Fudd's land has jumped in value ever since the rabbits ran riot over the neighborhood. How will this defense affect Fudd's case?

(A)   Fudd's case will probably fail, because he cannot show harm under either legal theory.

(B)   Fudd's case will probably collapse, because the court will find that the social utility of more rabbits outweighs the infringement on Fudd's property rights.

(C)   Fudd's case is stronger, because the appraisal confirms that the defendant let rabbits invade neighboring properties.

(D)   Fudd's remedies may be limited, but the defendant cannot avoid all liability.

63.   Which of the following is not an element of modern trespass actions?

(A)   A physical invasion affecting an interest in the exclusive possession of property.

(B)   An intentional doing of the act which results in the invasion.

(C)   Reasonable foreseeability that the act done would result in an invasion of plaintiff's possessory interest.

(D)   A showing of repeated invasions or intrusions, as opposed to a single, isolated incident.

64.   An old tannery in Woburn, MA buries toxic waste on its property for several decades, contaminating the wells in the area and causing the deaths of eight children and a high rate of other sicknesses. One of the property owners, having no family members who are at risk, brings a lawsuit against the tannery and the large corporate conglomerates that own shares in it, under a theory of public nuisance. What is the likely outcome of this civil action?

(A)   The case is so strong that he should win at the summary judgment phase, forcing the defendants to clean up the contamination and compensate all the victims.

(B)   The court will probably dismiss the action, because he will never be able to prove causation.

(C)   The court will probably dismiss the action, because private plaintiffs cannot bring public nuisance actions; these are the domain of state enforcement officials.

(D)   He will probably prevail, because public nuisance actions use a theory of strict liability, lowering the plaintiff's burden of proof.

65. The Red Cross, a nonprofit organization, wants to construct a series of emergency housing shelters along the Gulf Coast for victims of perennial hurricanes. One of the sites they select is near a natural wetland — and estuary where many rare species of birds nest to hatch their young. An activist group called Save the Eggs Already (SEA) challenges their proposed action under NEPA, in an attempt to force the Red Cross to complete an Environmental Impact Statement (EIS) before proceeding. What is the likely result of this litigation?

    (A) The court will order the Red Cross to halt the project until it completes an EIS.

    (B) The court will dismiss the action because NEPA applies only to governmental agencies, and the Red Cross is obviously a private nonprofit entity.

    (C) The court will order the Red Cross to complete an Environmental Assessment (EA) first to determine whether an EIS is necessary.

    (D) The court will dismiss the action because citizen groups lack standing under NEPA.

66. The Army Corps of Engineers is planning a significant building project (a bypass) that will have undeniable significant effects on the environment, and will cost hundreds of millions of dollars to complete. It has also planned precise mitigation measures to offset the harm to wildlife and the environment, compensating for it with nearby wildlife preserves, extra protections against other types of pollution and human activity in the area, etc. In fact, some experts believe the wildlife in the area will be better off after the project is complete. As a result, the Army Corps completes an Environmental Assessment (EA) and reaches a Finding of No Significant Impact (FONSI), and refuses to complete a more extensive Environmental Impact Statement (EIS). A few concerned environmentalists organize an opposition group called Against Contaminating the Human Environment ("A.C.H.E."), saying that an EIS is necessary because this is a major federal project that will significantly effect the environment. What is the likely outcome of this litigation?

    (A) A court will probably halt the project until the Army Corps completes an EIS.

    (B) A court will probably deny relief to the A.C.H.E. group because of the rigorous plans for mitigation.

    (C) A court will probably require the Army Corps do complete an "Assessment Review," and intermediate step between an EA and an EIS, to determine whether the proposed mitigation measures will be efficacious.

(D)   A court will probably deny relief to the A.C.H.E. group because the Army Corps of Engineers is always exempt from NEPA's requirements.

67.   The Army Corps of Engineers decides to cope with post-hurricane flooding by constructing enormous, twenty-story hot air blowers (similar to a gigantic hair dryer) all along the Gulf Coast, which can evaporate thousands of gallons of water from flooded towns and cities. Assume that NEPA applies here, and that the Army Corps completes a detailed Environmental Impact Statement laying out the possible effects of blowing huge gusts of scorching hot air over the surface of the flooded areas. The EIS mentions other alternatives in passing, such as managing flooding with systems of levies, sea walls, underground drainage channels, etc., but dismisses each of these as "expensive" and "old-fashioned." A group of angry activists called A.N.G.E.R. ("Against Negligent Government and Environmental Ruin") brings an action to enjoin the project under NEPA, saying the Army Corps failed to consider reasonable alternatives to the crackpot idea of installing behemoth hair dryers all along the Gulf Coast. The Army Corps contends that they considered and rejected all possible alternatives in the EIS already. What is the likely outcome in court?

(A)   A court will probably side with the Army Corps as long as it cites some serious scientific studies in rejecting the alternatives to the proposed project.

(B)   A court will probably side with the Army Corps because of NEPA's presumption in favor of innovative technology or techniques.

(C)   A court will probably side with A.N.G.E.R. and require the Army Corps to complete an Environmental Assessment (EA) first to determine whether a more comprehensive EIS is necessary.

(D)   A court will probably side with A.N.G.E.R. and require the Army Corps to complete a revised EIS that gives more serious consideration to traditional, widely-used alternatives to the more radical proposed project.

68.   The federal Economics and Statistics Administration (ESA) wants to avoid doing lengthy, costly Environmental Impact Statements (EIS's) as much as possible. It therefore promulgates regulations exempting many specific types of its regular activities from NEPA's requirements. What is the common term for these exemptions?

(A)   "Categorical exclusions."

(B)   "Criteria exclusions."

(C)   "Statutory exclusions."

(D)   "Project Scoping."

69.   The National Nuclear Security Administration (NNSA), through its subsidiary Office of Fissile Materials Disposition (OMFD), creates a program to dispose of surplus

plutonium by downgrading it (diluting it significantly) at a special facility in rural Kentucky. A handful of residents in that area band together to protest the construction of the facility, fearing it will cause their family members and farm animals to develop cancer and other diseases. The NNSA and OFMD completed a thorough Environmental Impact Statement (EIS) already, with extremely detailed consideration of all possible physical effects from the operation of the facility or even foreseeable accidents or mishaps that may occur. The concerned residents challenge the EIS in court, arguing that it fails to consider the psychological impact on the residents, their families, and their farm animals if this facility is built. How will the court respond to this argument?

(A)   A court will probably order the agency to reopen the EIS, but only to consider this particular aspect.

(B)   A court will probably side with the agency and hold that mere psychological effects are not required areas for analysis under NEPA.

(C)   A court will probably order the agency to complete an Environmental Assessment (EA) to determine whether the EIS should be reopened.

(D)   A court will find that the psychological concerns of the residents constitute a "social controversy" under CEQ guidelines, and should be included in a revised EIS.

70.   What is probably the most commonly-litigated requirement under in NEPA?

(A)   The requirement that federal agencies refrain from harming the environment more than is "reasonably necessary."

(B)   The requirement that federal agencies complete and Environmental Impact Statement about major projects.

(C)   The requirement that the Council on Environmental Quality (CEQ) review and approve Environmental Impact Statements.

(D)   The requirement that federal projects protect endangered species more than humans.

71.   The Department of Transportation wants to build a high-speed bullet train in Texas from Laredo to Lubbock, to accommodate daily commuters between those two cities. The Department dutifully prepares an Environmental Impact Statement (EIS), which considers all the environmental effects, possible alternatives, and the costs and benefits of completing the project. There are no clear alternatives for transporting large numbers of commuters across arid terrain over such great distances. Nevertheless, the EIS concludes that the project will have a devastating permanent effect on the environment of western Texas. An activist group called Don't Mess With Texas (DMWT) commences litigation under NEPA Sec. 102(2)(c), to force the EPA to stop the plan

because its environmental impact outweighs the purported benefits. How would a court respond?

(A)   The court will dismiss the action because NEPA gives no authority to the EPA to stop projects because of the environmental impact suggested in the EIS.

(B)   The court will enjoin the plan because it does not meet NEPA's "reasonableness" standard.

(C)   The court's response will depend on whose environmental experts are more convincing, the agency's or the activists'.

(D)   The court will dismiss the action because DMWT lacks standing under NEPA to challenge a proposed action.

72.   Courtney is a new project manager at the Grain Inspection, Packers and Stockyard Administration (GIPSA), a federal agency operating as a division of the Department of Agriculture. The Administrator has assigned Courtney the responsibility for preparing an Environmental Assessment (EA) to comply with NEPA for a new project GIPSA is starting. Courtney is not sure how long the final EA should be, or how much time this will require. What is the typical length for an EA?

(A)   1–5 pages.

(B)   10–15 pages.

(C)   100–150 pages.

(D)   1000–15,000 pages.

73.   The federal Administration on Aging wants to build a new regional office building in Boca Raton, Florida. Before beginning construction, the Administration complies with NEPA and completes an Environmental Assessment (EA) to determine whether the project would have significant impact on the human environment, and reasonably concludes that it will not. What is the common term for this type of conclusion?

(A)   Self-aggrandizing political grandstanding.

(B)   NEPA Final Ruling.

(C)   "Project Scoping."

(D)   Finding of No Significant Impact (FONSI).

74.   The Texas Secretary of State wants to construct a new satellite office in Corsicana, an old town between Houston and Dallas. The building will cost several million dollars and will be on lovely riverfront property, so there is little question that this is a "major" government action that could have a "significant" effect on the environment. A group of

disgruntled local residents opposes to construction, and bands together to form an opposition group called Corsicanans Revolting Against Politicians (C.R.A.P.). This activist group challenges the agency plans in court, contending that the agency should have to complete and EIS before proceeding. The Secretary is confident that NEPA does not apply. What is the likely outcome of this case?

(A)   The Secretary of State will have to complete an EIS, but may be permitted to continue with the project in the meantime.

(B)   The Secretary will have to complete an Environmental Assessment (EA) to demonstrate that an EIS is unnecessary.

(C)   The Secretary is correct that NEPA is inapplicable, as long as this is a state action and there is no federal involvement.

(D)   The Secretary is correct that NEPA is inapplicable, because NEPA does not apply to the construction of government office buildings.

75.   What federal agency promulgates standards, requirements, and guidelines for the implementation of NEPA?

(A)   The National Fish & Wildlife Service.

(B)   The Environmental Protection Agency.

(C)   The Council on Environmental Quality.

(D)   The Army Corps of Engineers.

76.   The EPA wants to create a new large-scale program to auction off pollution rights for generators of toxic wastes, based on the success of its pollution auctions under the Clean Air Act. An activist group named No More Auctions (NMA) sues to prevent the EPA from proceeding until it completes an Environmental Impact Statement (EIS) about the possible effects on the human environment from this new program. The EPA refuses to complete an EIS. What is the likely result in court?

(A)   The EPA will probably prevail, because courts have held that NEPA generally does not apply to the EPA.

(B)   The EPA will have to complete an EIS, but they may be permitted to continue with the project in the meantime.

(C)   The EPA will have to complete an Environmental Assessment (EA) to demonstrate that an EIS is unnecessary.

(D)   The court will dismiss the action because NEPA does not give standing to activist groups.

77. Cody is a new project manager at the Administration for Children and Families (ACF) in Washington, D.C. His supervisor has placed him in charge of a small team preparing an Environmental Impact Statement (EIS) for a new project of stockpiling millions of doses of influenza vaccines in strategic locations around the country in case of a pandemic. Cody is not sure how long the EIS should be or how much time this project will require. What is the typical length for a completed EIS?

    (A) 20–80 pages.

    (B) 200–800 pages.

    (C) 2000–8000 pages.

    (D) 20,000–80,000 pages.

78. What requirements does NEPA place on federal agencies to mitigate the adverse environmental effects of a proposed project identified in the Environmental Impact Statement (EIS)?

    (A) The agency must take mitigation measures that have a precise, one-to-one correspondence with each adverse effect of the proposed plan.

    (B) The agency can avail itself of NEPA's "functional equivalence" rule, and have mitigation measures that roughly offset the deleterious effects described in the EIS.

    (C) NEPA itself does not require federal agencies to have any mitigation plans.

    (D) NEPA requires no mitigation from the agency proposing the project; instead, the EPA must propose mitigation measures.

79. The federal Department of Housing and Urban Development (HUD) needs to clear some tree branches, and brush that has overgrown a corner of its parking lot at a regional headquarters office. It also needs to repair some deep potholes in the corner parking space now covered by brush and brambles. Although this represents only a day of labor by the building maintenance crew, several species of rare (but not endangered) birds have nested in the overgrown foliage and are sitting on eggs. In addition, the potholes, which always contain some standing water, have become the home for a previously-undiscovered species of salamander. The other problem with this parking space is that the pavement pitches away from the rest of the parking lot, into a deep ravine that runs directly into a nearby estuary. Any toxic fluids dropping or leaking from cars parked there will wash into the estuary every time it rains. There is little question that making the parking space usable for cars will have some serious environmental impact, but no one is sure of the extent of the harm that will result. Learning of HUD's final plans to clear the parking space from overgrown foliage and repair the potholes, a local environmentalist group, called No Additional Parking Spaces ("N.A.P.S.") challenges

the agency in court, saying it should comply with NEPA requirements and complete an Environmental Impact Statement (EIS). What is the likely outcome of this case?

(A) A court will probably order HUD to complete an Environmental Assessment (EA) to determine if an EIS is necessary.

(B) A court will probably order HUD to complete and EIS before clearing the corner of the parking lot.

(C) A court will probably rule against N.A.P.S. on the ground that this is not a "major" federal action and therefore NEPA does not require an EIS.

(D) A court will probably rule against N.A.P.S. on the ground that it lacks standing.

80. A federal agency called the Office of Civilian Radioactive Waste Management (OCRWM) wants to create a disposal site for used building materials and office rubbish from nuclear facilities — garbage that has elevated levels of radioactivity from long-term exposure to radiation. The waste is not itself radioactive waste material. The agency has selected a location in a completely unpopulated desert for the site. Agency officials refuse to expend taxpayer dollars on an expensive Environmental Impact Statement (EIS), asserting that the project will not significantly affect the quality of the human environment because no one lives within a hundred miles of the site. Under NEPA, must the federal agency undertake some environmental review or assessment, even if it appears to everyone that effects are humans are unlikely?

(A) No, NEPA applies only where significant effects on the human environment are self-evident.

(B) No, NEPA applies only to the EPA, not to obscure agencies like this one.

(C) Yes, the agency must automatically complete an Environmental Impact Statement for serious hazards like radioactive waste.

(D) Yes, the agency must do some preliminary investigation and assessment to establish that there is not likely to be any effect on the human environment.

81. Which of the following best describes NEPA's primary purpose?

(A) NEPA should prevent the federal government from devastating the environment through agency-sponsored projects.

(B) NEPA should give the EPA greater control over other government agencies regarding projects that could effect the human environment.

(C) NEPA should forces agencies to obtain information about the environmental impact of proposed government projects.

(D)   NEPA pre-empts common law nuisance claims against federal agencies for projects that harm neighboring properties.

82.   Which of the following is not one of NEPA's primary effects?

(A)   NEPA has forced federal agencies to rethink many projects, and sometimes their agency's overall mission.

(B)   NEPA has empowered activist groups with a powerful litigation tool for stalling governmental projects on procedural technicalities.

(C)   NEPA has made major governmental projects more expensive for taxpayers.

(D)   NEPA has protected countless animal species from extinction.

83.   The Federal Energy Regulatory Commission (FERC) has a major project in view but wants to avoid the lengthy and costly process of completing an Environmental Impact Statement (EIS). To avoid the classification of a "major" project with a "significant" impact on the environment, agency bureaucrats cleverly break the project into many smaller, seemingly unrelated projects, all of which safely avoid the dreaded classifications under NEPA. What is the common term for this strategy?

(A)   "Environmental gerrymandering."

(B)   "FONSI" (Finding of No Significant Impact).

(C)   "Project Scoping."

(D)   "Eutrophication."

84.   Congress creates a new federal agency to study and prevent bioterrorism attacks. Knowing that the agency will need to conduct dangerous experiments and tests, it wants to shield the agency from the tedious requirements of NEPA. Which of the following is the best way to achieve this goal?

(A)   Congress should order the agency to break all its projects into smaller pieces that evade the classification of "major government project."

(B)   Congress should simply include a statutory exemption from NEPA's requirements in the enabling statute for the agency.

(C)   Congress should set the agency's budget low enough to avoid the classification of "major government project."

(D)   Congress should statutorily deny standing to activist groups that would bring NEPA enforcement actions.

85.   Bob is the new director of the National Rural Development Partnership (NRDP), a division of the Department of Agriculture. During a lunch conversation with his

subordinates, someone suggests, "We could help poor farmers if we built free grain silos for them." Several people nodded in agreement and went on with their lunch. Bob mentioned three possible sites in his hometown in Mississippi that would be good candidates for such a project. A disgruntled employee who was present at the lunch leaks the conversation to the press, who begin to run stories about the possible project. An environmentalist group called No More Silos (NMS) sues under NEPA for Bob's failure to complete an Environmental Assessment (EA), much less and Environmental Impact Statement (EIS). What is the likely result of the litigation?

(A)   The court is likely to ask the NRDP to complete an Environmental Assessment (EA) to determine whether the EIS should be completed.

(B)   The court is likely to reject the environmental group's claims, because NEPA applies only to "projects," and this appears to be a tentative idea, not a "proposal" or a "project."

(C)   The court is likely to order the NRDP to complete and EIS, but may allow them to continue with the project in the meantime.

(D)   The court will dismiss the action because the citizens lack standing, because the case is not yet ripe.

86.   The Food and Drug Administration (FDA) needs to expand its regional offices to have much larger waiting rooms for representatives of pharmaceutical companies that are seeking approval for new, beneficial drugs. Many of the locations will require new construction to add the waiting room space, with undeniable physical effects on the nearby environment. In addition, however, the expansive waiting rooms will mean more automobile traffic and parked cars around the regional offices, more frustrated company representatives loitering around outside, many more cell phones being used to communicate with representatives to call their home office to check for messages. It is foreseeable that the expanded waiting centers will attract more unattractive snack shops, convenience stores, and newspaper stands to service the growing number of people waiting there. Finally, area residents will become more aware of the chronic delays in approval for new drugs, which instills a sense of depression, frustration, and fear of contracting a disease for which a cure is known but unavailable. The FDA completes an EIS for the project, but considers only the physical environmental effects of the construction projects. A group of concerned citizens organizes, calling itself R.O.L.F.D.A. ("Resist Overwhelming Lines at the FDA"), and contends in court that the EIS should consider social and psychological effects of the proposed project, not just the immediate physical effects. What is the likely judicial response to this argument?

(A)   A court will probably order the agency to reopen the EIS, but only to consider this particular aspect.

(B)   A court will probably side with the agency and hold that mere social or psychological effects are not required areas for analysis under NEPA.

(C)   A court will probably order the agency to complete an Environmental Assessment (EA) to determine whether the EIS should be reopened.

(D)   A court will find that the FDA is always exempt from NEPA.

87.   Assume the facts above about the FDA's expansion of its luxurious waiting rooms, but now assume that the FDA found ways to utilize existing space within its buildings more efficiently, so there will be no new construction and no demonstrable effects on the physical environment around the buildings. The amount of waiting space will be increased to the same extent, however, and all the potential social and psychological harms will still ensue. The same citizen group, ROLFDA, litigates over the EIS, claiming it should have considered these effects. How would this change in the facts alter the outcome of the case?

(A)   There would be no significant change in the outcome of the case, because the court would still order the agency to consider these social and psychological harms as part of the "human environment."

(B)   There would be a significant change in the outcome of the case, because the court will be more concerned about a project whose entire harm is social and psychological, unmitigated by physical harm.

(C)   There would be a significant change in the outcome of the case, as the court will probably consider the social and psychological effects only if there is also some potential physical harm to the environment.

(D)   There would be no significant change in the outcome of the case, because the court will probably order the agency to complete an Environmental Assessment (EA) to determine whether the EIS should be reopened.

88.   Alice is the new director for the Center for Nutrition Policy and Promotion, a division of the Department of Agriculture. For one of her agency's major projects, they have completed a draft Environmental Impact Statement (EIS). Alice is not sure how or where to publish the document. Where does the agency publish a draft EIS?

(A)   In the local newspaper in the areas likely to be affected by the proposed project.

(B)   On the agency's website.

(C)   In the Federal Register.

(D)   In the Federal Appendix.

89. The Federal Aviation Administration (FAA) wants to conduct tests on the feasibility of jetliners making emergency crash landings in national parklands in the event of attempted hijackings. The proposed testing project involves crashing about fifty full-sized jetliners (without passengers) into designated federal parks or forests in the Midwest. The FAA completed a thorough Environmental Impact Statement (EIS), defeated some initial NEPA challenges in court, and is proceeding with its plan. A student activist group called "No More Crashes" (NMC) then discovers that one of the designated crash sites has a number of natural springs tapping into an enormous underground aquifer that was previously unknown. NMC sues the FAA to compel the agency to reopen its EIS and consider this newly discovered information about the environmental effects of the proposed action. What is the likely result?

(A) The court is likely to order the FAA to reopen its EIS and address the environmental effects of the project in light of this new information.

(B) The court is likely to ask the FAA to complete an Environmental Assessment (EA) to determine whether the EIS should be reopened.

(C) The court will dismiss the action because the EIS is complete and the decision is already final.

(D) The court will dismiss the action because the activist group lacks standing under NEPA.

90. How long does a state's SIP remain in force after it is approved by the EPA?

    (A) Until either the EPA or the state decides to adopt changes to the SIP.

    (B) Until the state attains the required NAAQS levels, at which point the SIP becomes moot.

    (C) Until both the EPA and the state agree to adopt changes to the SIP.

    (D) Until the statutory deadline expires.

91. Suppose Arizona procrastinates completing its SIP to the point of missing every federally-mandated deadline under the Clean Air Act. An environmentalist watchdog group that calls itself "Hurry Up!" brings suit to compel the agency to compel with federal law. What is the consequence of a state failing to adopt a SIP under the Clean Air Act?

ANSWER:

92. *Chevron*, purportedly the most-cited U.S. Supreme Court case of all time, was actually about the EPA's "bubble rule." The "bubble" was a way to get around what stricture of the Clean Air Act?

    (A) Infeasible emission standards for new construction of "stationary sources."

    (B) Infeasible emission standards for new automobiles and their "catalytic converters."

    (C) The unreasonable deadlines for states to adopt SIPs and comply with NAAQS.

    (D) The requirement that the EPA identify and regulate "criteria air pollutants" like lead (Pb) in the atmosphere.

93. After a major hurricane in the Gulf of Mexico damages some oil refineries in the region, intrepid reporter Clark Kent explains to millions of eager television viewers that "no new oil refineries have been built in America in over 30 years." To the extent this is true, it is due to:

    (A) CERCLA provisions about new construction.

(B)   CWA provisions about new construction.

(C)   RCRA provisions about new construction.

(D)   CAA provisions about new construction.

94.   One fallacy of such news commentary about "no new refineries being built for the last 30 years" is:

(A)   Nobody would want new refineries built here, anyway.

(B)   Under a (somewhat lenient) EPA interpretation, new facilities are not "new construction" as long as they are contiguous to old facilities that were grandfathered in — meaning that many refineries have new facilities but no "new" ones were built in a technical, legal sense.

(C)   There were no legal impediments to building new refineries during this entire period; the lack of construction simply reflects market forces and industry decisions about profitability.

(D)   This is just part of the propaganda war to fool the terrorists, so they will never discover the locations of our best refineries.

95.   Curious George has always wanted to see his state's complete SIP with his own eyes. Where does Curious George go to find the complete SIP for his state?

(A)   No one has ever seen a complete SIP; the SIP is never published as a complete work.

(B)   In a special volume of the Federal Appendix, which has a separate volume for each state in alphabetical order.

(C)   In the most recent Federal Register, where administrative agencies must publish every rule they promulgate.

(D)   To his state's official SIP website, fully indexed, which every state must have under the Freedom of Information Act.

96.   For purposes of the Clean Air Act, to what does the ubiquitous acronym SIP refer?

ANSWER:

97.   Abel is a new project manager at his state's environmental agency, in charge of a team that conducts detailed cost-benefit analysis for each state regulation promulgated by his agency. Abel is discovering that this seemingly straightforward task includes many

complicates and obstacles. Which of the following is NOT a problem with cost-benefit analysis?

(A)   The problem of future discounting, i.e., setting a discount rate.

(B)   The problem of valuing (in dollars) a human life.

(C)   The problem of selling it to the regulated industry.

(D)   The problem of quantifying aesthetic benefits and natural beauty.

98.   Judge Antonia Statist is a member of the Federalist Society, and she believes passionately in the rights of states to govern themselves, unhampered by federal intervention. Judge Statist's favorite topic of discussion is the Clean Air Act, which she views as an erosion of Constitutional limits on federal power; she believes every state should be free to make its own air pollution laws, without needing EPA approval. What is the best argument against Judge Statist's position?

(A)   Air pollution always drifts across state lines, creating an interstate problem with one state externalizing its pollution onto another.

(B)   We might end up with an array of different, even contradictory, laws in each state.

(C)   The states might discover their ability to govern themselves and revolt against more areas of federal regulation.

(D)   The states might do nothing to regulate air pollution, which would harm its own citizens.

99.   Vermont decides to lead the nation in reducing pollution from automobiles, so it adopts state regulations exactly twice as stringent as the EPA's regulations for automobile emissions, which Vermont regulators consider "wimpy." Vermont regulators celebrate the fact that they have finally surpassed California as the vanguard of environmentalism, at least in this area. The automobile industry, which feels it cannot economically comply with such radical new regulations, asks its most eloquent spokesperson to hold a press conference to hold a press conference, at which the spokesperson says just five words: "See you in court, Vermont!" Will Vermont's bold new regulations stand up in court?

(A)   Yes, as long as they are as strict — or stricter — than the federal regulations for the same pollutants.

(B)   No, because the Clean Air Act prohibits every state except California from enacting regulations stricter than the EPA's rules for these pollutants.

(C)   Yes, as long as Vermont includes these regulations as part of its SIP, and obtains approval from the EPA.

      (D)   No, because the existence of a federal statute automatically pre-empts all state environmental regulations of any kind.

100.   Assume the facts above about Vermont's new regulations for automobile emissions, but now assume that Vermont simply copied whatever regulations California was using at the time, and California had somewhat more stringent regulations than the EPA's rules. Given these changed facts, would Vermont's somewhat-less-bold new initiative stand up in court?

      (A)   No, because the existence of a federal statute automatically pre-empts all state environmental regulations of any kind.

      (B)   No, because the Clean Air Act permits only California to exceed federal regulations for automobile pollutants.

      (C)   Yes, because other states can require "mobile sources" to meet California's more stringent standards.

      (D)   Yes, but only if California grants Vermont permission to copy their regulations.

101.   What do we mean by a "technology-based standard" under the Clean Air Act?

      (A)   A regulation that dictates what type of device or technology a certain industry must use for pollution control on its smokestacks or exhaust pipes.

      (B)   A regulation that dictates what types of technology or industries are allowed to operate in a given area, based on how much air pollution such facilitates usually generate.

      (C)   A regulation that defines maximum "healthy" levels of pollutants in the ambient air and mandates that all stationary sources of those pollutants find ways to keep the ambient air within those levels.

      (D)   A regulation that uses the latest technology to determine maximum "healthy" levels of pollutants in the ambient air and to monitor ambient air quality.

102.   Section 111 of the Clean Air Act authorizes the EPA to promulgate limitations on the amount of air pollutants that "new or modified stationary sources" can emit. What is the technical name for these restrictions?

ANSWER:

103.   Judy is a new project manager at the EPA in its Air Pollution division. Her supervisor assigns her the task of determining the best "health-based standard" for carbon dioxide, which the EPA has never before regulated. Judy feels confused by the assignment. What

does the supervisor mean by a "health-based" regulation or standard under the Clean Air Act?

(A) A regulation that dictates what type of device or technology a certain industry must use for pollution control on its smokestacks or exhaust pipes.

(B) A regulation that dictates what types of technology or industries are allowed to operate in a given area, based on how much air pollution such facilitates usually generate.

(C) A regulation that defines maximum "healthy" levels of pollutants in the ambient air and mandates that all stationary sources of those pollutants find ways to keep the ambient air within those levels.

(D) A regulation that requires the latest technology to determine maximum "healthy" levels of pollutants in the ambient air and to monitor ambient air quality.

104. Under the Clean Air Act, the EPA has authority (or even a duty) to identify and regulate certain air pollutants as "criteria pollutants." What is the significance of the EPA designating an airborne substance as a "criteria pollutant"?

(A) There is a statutorily-mandated zero-tolerance rule for these pollutants, meaning no stationary or mobile source can emit any quantity, no mater how small.

(B) The EPA must conduct a cost-benefit analysis to determine the most economically feasible regulations for appropriate levels of the criteria pollutants in the ambient air.

(C) Any federal agency that contributes to levels of these criteria pollutants in the air must complete an Environmental Impact Statement (EIS) for relevant activities.

(D) The EPA must promulgate and enforce National Ambient Air Quality Standards (NAAQS) for each of these criteria pollutants.

105. In response to growing public concerns about "global warming," a group of student activists demands that the EPA designate carbon dioxide as a "criteria pollutant," so that limitations on emissions could come into effect for major urban areas. What other pollutants already have this designation?

(A) Hundreds, if we include the many "characteristic pollutants" that exhibit toxicity, ignitability, corrosiveness, and reactivity.

(B) Exactly 169, including most emissions from factories, automobiles, and municipal waste incinerators.

(C) None, because the EPA decided in the 1970s to regulate air pollutants through technology-based standards instead.

(D)   Six: ozone, particulate matter, sulfur oxides, carbon monoxide, nitrogen oxides and lead.

106.   Assume that in response to political pressure and litigation by various special interest groups, the EPA agrees to list carbon dioxide as a "criteria pollutant" to address global warming concerns. The EPA then promulgates regulations about the appropriate maximum levels for this criteria pollutant. What is the primary mechanism for implementing and enforcing these new standards?

(A)   The EPA will use technology-based standards to implement the new criteria pollutant regulations.

(B)   The Clean Air Act primarily utilizes permits and voluntary reporting requirements to implement regulations for criteria pollutants.

(C)   Each state's SIP will have to include a detailed plan for attaining the required levels of carbon dioxide in the ambient air.

(D)   The primary enforcement mechanism will be citizen suits brought by environmental watchdog groups.

107.   Assume that the EPA lists carbon dioxide as a criteria pollutant, promulgates the necessary regulations, and devises an appropriate implementation mechanism. Even so, Los Angeles, Chicago, Houston, and New York City all fail miserably at meeting the standards. What will be the legal consequence of this failure?

(A)   The EPA will use its "bubble rule" to smooth over the problem, putting an imaginary bubble over the respective states as a whole, so that urban pollution is offset by unpolluted rural areas.

(B)   These cities will receive the designation "non-attainment zone" and will face special burdensome restrictions about new construction of pollution sources and reductions by existing sources.

(C)   The EPA will have to create a Federal Implementation Plan (FIP) in place of the state's SIP, at least for these areas.

(D)   Courts will invalidate the regulations because their infeasibility violates the "arbitrary and capricious" standard for judicial review of agency actions.

108.   How often does the EPA add substances to the list of "criteria pollutants"?

(A)   Not since 1978, when the EPA added lead (Pb) to the list.

(B)   The EPA constantly tinkers with the list, adding and removing substances, publishing each proposed change in the Federal Register.

(C)   Whenever there is a public outcry or political pressure to reduce the levels of some pollutant in the ambient air.

(D)   Every five years, as mandated by the Clean Air Act.

109.   "Smog" is the common term for which of the criteria pollutants?

ANSWER:

110.   "Acid rain" is mostly associated with which of the following criteria pollutants?

ANSWER:

111.   The vast areas of west Texas remain largely unpopulated and have relatively low levels of criteria pollutants in the ambient air. Assume the air is actually cleaner than what is required by the NAAQS. To preserve this happy situation, what special programs or regulations is the EPA likely to impose there?

(A)   No further burdens or restrictions will be imposed on this area.

(B)   The NAAQS program for normal-attainment areas and "Reasonably Available Control Technology" for existing stationary sources.

(C)   The Prevention of Significant Deterioration (PSD) program and "Best Available Control Technologies" (BACT) for new stationary sources.

(D)   "Lowest Achievable Emission Rates" (LAER) for existing stationary sources.

112.   Curious George becomes the Governor of a major industrial state, and he governs as a virtual autocrat, demanding and intolerant. George believes environmental regulations are stifling business and economic development in his state, and one day he demands to see the state's SIP, in its entirety, at the Governor's Mansion. His loyal subjects at first try to send him on a wild goose chase in the local public library, but eventually they attempt to comply with this unprecedented request. What would be the most practical way to deliver the entire SIP to the Governor's Mansion?

(A)   In a letter-sized envelope.

(B)   In a box full of file folders.

(C)   With a forklift carrying several boxes bound together on a warehouse pallet.

(D)   In a convoy of tractor-trailer trucks.

113. Sally owns an old industrial facility that emits large quantities of gaseous toluene, which the EPA decides to list as a "Hazardous Air Pollutant" (HAP). What kind of regulations will Sally face for emissions of HAPs?

(A) Technology-based limits based on Maximum Available Control Technology (MACT).

(B) Health-based limits based on the NAAQS for this pollutant.

(C) Permit requirements that involve lengthy, direct negotiations with EPA officials.

(D) Technology and health-based limits, including Reasonable Air Control Technology (RACT).

114. Cody runs several businesses, including an older facility that puts lots of sulfur dioxide into the atmosphere. He obtains the standard "allowance" for emitting one ton of sulfur dioxide per year into the air. Cody decides the facility is not very profitable, and that he could make more money if he scales back operations and sells his allowance to a competitor who has a more successful plant. What would be the legal consequences if this sale were discovered?

(A) Cody could face fines of $25,000 per day, and even jail time, for willfully trying to circumvent the provisions of Clean Air Act.

(B) Nothing, because the EPA intends sulfur dioxide allowances to be transferable.

(C) Cody could face a (costly) citizen suit by environmental activists seeking to enjoin him to comply with the Clean Air Act.

(D) Cody will find state regulators are less cooperative with him about his other businesses complying with the state SIP.

115. Vermont decides to lead the nation in reducing water pollution, so it adopts state regulations exactly twice as stringent as the EPA's regulations for point source discharges, which Vermont regulators consider "wimpy." Vermont regulators celebrate the fact that they have finally surpassed all other states as the vanguard of environmentalism, at least in this area. The affected industry, which feels it cannot economically comply with such radical new regulations, asks its most eloquent spokesperson to hold a press conference to hold a press conference, at which the spokesperson says just five words: "See you in court, Vermont!" Will Vermont's bold new regulations stand up in court?

   (A) No, because the Clean Water Act prohibits every state except California from enacting regulations stricter than the EPA's rules for these pollutants.

   (B) Yes, as long as Vermont includes these regulations as part of its SIP, and obtains approval from the EPA.

   (C) Yes, as long as they are as strict — or stricter — than the federal regulations for the same pollutants.

   (D) No, because the existence of a federal statute automatically pre-empts all state environmental regulations of any kind.

116. An "estuary" is:

   (A) A type of pollution-control mechanism on smokestacks.

   (B) A place where fresh water and ocean water mix, and an essential breeding ground for many wild animals and fish.

   (C) A linguistic device emphasized by Justice Scalia.

   (D) An endangered species, responsible for halting the multimillion-dollar dam project in *TVA v. Hill.*

117. Sarah gets a job at the state environmental agency in their Water Permit Department. Her job is to review permit applications and issue the appropriate permit for the situation. She finds a host of abbreviations used constantly: BMP, BPT, BCT, BAT, and BDAT, and she has trouble keeping them straight because they all start with the same letter and all end with the same letter, except for one, BMP. She decides to start by

mastering the one that ends with a different letter than the others. What is "BMP," for purposes of the Clean Water Act?

ANSWER:

118.   Continuing from the question above, "BPT" in environmental law is an abbreviation for:

ANSWER:

119.   Continuing from the question above, what is "BCT" in environmental law?

ANSWER:

120.   Continuing the series of questions about Sarah needing to learn the most common abbreviations used for water permits, what is "BAT," for purposes of the Clean Water Act?

ANSWER:

121.   This is the next question in this series about the confusing abbreviations for the Clean Water Act: "BDAT" in environmental law is an abbreviation for:

ANSWER:

122. Sarah, the new permit application reviewer at the state environmental agency, is ready to arrange the mysterious abbreviations in order of relative strictness. What is the relative stringency of the foregoing abbreviations (from least stringent to most)?

ANSWER:

123. Sarah notices one term that comes up frequently in Clean Water Act litigation is "practicable" as in "Best Practicable Technology." At first glance, she thought the word said "practical," but now she notices the extra syllable. What is the difference between "practicable" and "practical"?

(A) The two words are synonyms — "practicable" is simply and archaic spelling variant of "practical."

(B) "Practicable" means something one might practice over time; "practical" means "useful" or "effective."

(C) "Practicable" is a technical term referring only to financial feasibility (affordability); "practical" means "pragmatic," "useful," or "effective."

(D) "Practical" is a technical term referring only to financial feasibility (affordability); "practicable" means "pragmatic," "useful," or "effective."

124. Which of the B_ _ abbreviations (BDAT, BCT, BAT, etc.) applies to most toxic substances discharged into the waterways?

ANSWER:

125. Peter the Prosecutor lives in El Paso, which has a remarkably low crime rate. As a prosecutor, Peter finds himself with nothing to do for days at a time, and wants to start pursuing some environmental criminal enforcement to beef up his docket. He asks around and learns that most of the environmental criminal prosecutions are brought under provisions of RCRA for hazardous waste dumping. After RCRA, which major environmental statute gives rise to the most environmental criminal prosecutions?

(A) Clean Water Act.

(B) Clean Air Act.

(C) NEPA.

(D) FIFRA.

126. Peter the Environmental Prosecutor does not want to spend his time on petty crimes or small fines. He needs to focus on big-dollar fines and serious jail time for his defendants, because such cases attract more media attention for his office, and (directly and indirectly) boost his career. What types of penalties does Peter have at his disposal under Sec. 309(c) of the Clean Water Act for "negligent" violations?

ANSWER:

127. Jeffrey operates an industrial facility, which occasionally power-washes corroded or encrusted machinery with solvents on an asphalt patio between two of its buildings. The pools of spent solvents are mopped up, but residue remains in the asphalt. When it rains, the rainwater from the patio collects in natural gullies or trenches on-site before draining into a local stream. What kind of permit will Jeffrey need to obtain for this storm water runoff?

(A) No permit, because the collection trenches are on his own property.

(B) No permit, because the discharge happens only when it rains, and the rainwater is natural.

(C) Jeffrey needs to obtain an NAAQS permit for the storm water discharge.

(D) The facility should obtain an NPDES permit that covers storm water runoff.

128. The famous Milwaukee II case involved tons of raw sewage from Wisconsin washing up on the beaches of Chicago. Why did the Illinois plaintiffs have no judicial recourse to stop the nuisance?

(A) The Clean Water Act pre-empted federal common law for water-borne nuisances, and the Milwaukee sewage discharge was within the legal parameters of the CWA.

(B) The plaintiffs lacked standing to pursue their claim under the Clean Water Act.

(C) The statute of limitations had expired under the Clean Water Act.

(D) The discovery of the endangered "snail darter" among the sewage invoked the Endangered Species Act and forestalled any remedial actions.

129. What is an "effluent limitation" under the Clean Water Act?

(A) "Effluent limitations" are the diminutions in the flow of river water caused by industrial facilities redirecting some of the water through their plants.

(B) "Effluent limitations" are limits on the quantity or concentration of pollutants that some point source may discharge.

(C) "Effluent limitations" are limits on the discharge of municipal sewage treatment waste water back into a river.

(D) "Effluent limitations" are limits on the viscosity of liquids (how easily or quickly they flow) that are discharged into the environment.

130. Under the Clean Water Act, what is the difference between "technology-based standards" and "water quality standards"?

(A) Technology-based standards pertain to the type of pollution control devices and gadgets that polluters must deploy under their permits; water-quality standards pertain to the purity or contamination levels of the water in the river itself.

(B) Technology-based standards pertain to the types of technology or industry permitted to operate near a waterway, and water-quality standards refer to the contamination level of the water being discharged by a facility.

(C) Water-quality standards pertain to the type of pollution control devices and gadgets that polluters must deploy under their permits; technology-based standards pertain to the purity or contamination levels of the water in the river itself.

(D) Technology-based standards pertain to pollution-control devices and gadgets deployed by polluters, and water-quality standards pertain to the contamination levels in the effluent discharges themselves.

131. "Eutrophication" refers to:

ANSWER:

132. Intrepid attorney Perry Mason discovers that the murder victim in his case, who was the owner of a factory near the local river, obtained a "point source" NPDES permit for his site immediately before his untimely death. Perry Mason has not yet visited the factory site, but using his powers of deduction and the existence of a "point source" permit, he knows that somewhere on the property he will find something in particular. What does Perry Mason expect to find there?

(A) The source of a substantial amount of pollution concentrated at one point.

(B) An open pipe or drainage ditch that flows from the facility into navigable waters.

(C) A source for information that points to the killer.

(D) A sloping hill where rain water runs into navigable waters, carrying anything that has spilled on the surface with it.

133. Perry Mason suspects the victim's killer is a gardener at Southview Estate who was being blackmailed by the victim, a local factory owner. Attorney Mason finds during his investigation that the state environmental agency has long considered Southview Estate a "nonpoint source." Using his rapacious wit and powers of deduction, what can Perry Mason infer about Southview Estate?

(A) Somewhere on the property, there is an open pipe or drainage ditch that flows from the facility into navigable waters.

(B) He will find there a willing source of information for his case, but the information will point nowhere.

(C) The Estate includes open fields for grazing or crops, which generate significant amounts of rainwater runoff, contaminated with fertilizer, pesticides, herbicides, and animal manure.

(D) A toxic waste dump that is slowly leaching into the local water supply.

134. What are the typical water-quality standards of measure under the Clean Water Act?

ANSWER:

135. What term does the Clean Water Act use for municipal sewage treatment systems, and what regulations apply?

(A) Publicly Owned Treatment Works (or "POTWs"), and sources discharging into them are subject to the "pretreatment program."

(B) Municipal Sewage Treatment Plants (or "MSTPs"), and sources discharging into them are subject to the "pretreatment program."

(C) Nonpoint Sources, and no one is allowed to discharge into them except government entities.

(D) Point sources and anyone can discharge into them with a permit from the EPA.

136. Regarding criminal penalties for RCRA environmental violations, the question of law that often becomes the focus for the courts is the definitions of the word:

   (A) "Willfully."

   (B) "Pollutes."

   (C) "Knowingly."

   (D) "Federalism."

137. Sec. 3008(d) of RCRA, which is the focus of the famous *Laughlin* case, punishes intentional violations with up to:

   (A) $50,000 in fines for each day of violation, and five years imprisonment.

   (B) $25,000 in fines for each day of violation and up to one year imprisonment.

   (C) $50,000 in fines without imprisonment.

   (D) $20,000 in fines and up to three years imprisonment.

138. Criminal enforcement of RCRA currently favors prosecution of individuals instead of corporate entities. What is the name of the legal doctrine for this?

   (A) Piercing the Corporate Veil.

   (B) Vicarious Liability.

   (C) Responsible Corporate Officer.

   (D) Master-Servant Liability.

139. Acme Rocket Company is a "generator" for purposes of RCRA, because their factory produces several hazardous wastes that they must send to an off-site Temporary Storage Disposal Facility (TSDF). Once Acme has shipped the waste for disposal to the TSDF, does Acme have any more liability or obligation under RCRA?

ANSWER:

140.   What are the two ways that solid waste can be classified as a hazardous waste under RCRA?

ANSWER:

141.   Sweatshop, Inc. produces kryptonite hydroxide as a by-product of its other manufacturing. Suppose the EPA has "listed" kryptonite hydroxide as a hazardous substance under RCRA. The company conducts its own tests and concludes the substance poses absolutely no threat to human life. What is the company's legal recourse?

   (A)   They can produce it and ignore the EPA.

   (B)   They can challenge the EPA's statutory authority to make this decision.

   (C)   They can argue in court that it is neither ignitable, nor reactive, nor toxic, nor corrosive.

   (D)   They are pretty much out of luck if it is "listed."

142.   Dorkusmorkus Corp. has some "listed" hazardous waste left over from manufacturing a million little Dorkusmorkus widgets, a tiny tool for removing the stringy veins from celery stalks and replacing them with threads of delicious cream cheese. Dorkusmorkus learns that it is ridiculously expensive to dispose of "listed" wastes legally, so the managers decide to mix it into several tons of sand that they have in heaps on their property. They use enough so that the new mixture of slightly-green sand is basically harmless — it is not corrosive, ignitable, reactive, or toxic. Dorkusmorkus then gives the sand to building contractors who need it for mixing into concrete. Under RCRA, is the sand mixture a "hazardous" waste?

   (A)   No, because RCRA does not classify mixtures of "listed" hazardous waste and inert matter as "hazardous" waste, as long as the mixture does not exhibit one of the four hazardous characteristics.

   (B)   Yes, because RCRA contains special provisions about sand that is mixed into concrete.

   (C)   Yes, RCRA classifies such mixtures of "listed" hazardous waste and non-hazardous waste as "hazardous" waste, even if the mixture does not exhibit one of the four hazardous characteristics.

   (D)   No, because the company gives away the sand for free instead of sending it to a landfill.

143.   Sludgemonger Corporation makes a special fuel additive for lawn mower engines that enables the lawn mowers to go incredibly fast, at least for a few minutes at a time. Its leftover waste from manufacturing this liquid is a sludge that is highly flammable, but does not contain any "listed" substances under RCRA. Sludgemonger finds that proper disposal of this waste product is not affordable, so the managers decide to stir it into several tons of sand, which they found in heaps on a neighboring company's property. The company then sells this slightly-tainted sand to a third-world despot who has an endless need for sand to mix into the concrete for his underground bunkers. They use enough sand that the final mixed product is harmless and doesn't even burn when put in a furnace. How would RCRA classify this mixed product?

   (A)   It is hazardous waste because the final destination and use of the product is against American interests and public policy.

   (B)   The mixture is not considered hazardous waste, because RCRA classifies mixtures of "characteristic" hazardous waste and inert matter as non-hazardous waste, as long as the resulting mixture does not exhibit one of the four hazardous characteristics.

   (C)   It is not hazardous waste because the company sold it instead of dumping it.

   (D)   Sludgemonger has a problem: the mixture is still considered hazardous waste, because RCRA classifies mixtures of "characteristic" hazardous waste and inert matter as "hazardous" waste, even though the resulting mixture does not exhibit one of the four hazardous characteristics.

144.   Doofus, Inc. pumps water from a well to use at its "touchless" car wash. The well water, however, contains alarming levels of Heptachlor, a hazardous waste. The EPA insists the water itself is now hazardous waste. The rule for this categorization is usually called:

   (A)   The Contained-In Rule.

   (B)   The Derived-From Rule.

   (C)   The Mix-In Rule.

   (D)   The *Chevron* Rule.

145.   Play It Again, Inc. recycles commercial study aids dumped by law students after they graduate. Suppose that some of the study aids contain "listed" substances, either in the paper (to prevent it from turning yellow with age) or in the ink (to prevent you from licking the pages in your study aids). After grinding thousands of these used paperbacks into a pulp and producing recycled blank paper to sell back to the original publisher, Play It Again assumes that its recycled paper (which contains all the elements of the original) is not "waste" because it has been recycled into a useful product for resale. What will the EPA say about this?

(A)   The EPA will be impressed with their recycling efforts and the positive environmental impact.

(B)   The EPA has no authority under RCRA to regulate recycled materials, because RCRA applies only to "waste."

(C)   The EPA contends that it has authority under RCRA to regulate recycled materials in most cases, even where the recycler contends nothing is "wasted" because it is all eventually recycled.

(D)   The EPA will never know.

146.   Disappearance Corp. has a few barrels of hazardous waste left over from its operations at the end of every month. One of its warehouse workers has a pickup truck, and as a favor to his boss, loads up the barrels on the last day of every month and drives away with them; the barrels are never seen again. During a routine investigation, the EPA realizes some hazardous waste is coming from Disappearance's operations and asks to see the most recent "manifest." What is a "manifest," for purposes of EPA enforcement under RCRA?

(A)   The company's "Corporate Vision" or "Corporate Purpose" statement, which must include verbiage about being environmentally sensitive.

(B)   An annual report filed with the EPA about how much hazardous waste the company produced.

(C)   A special document, signed by the generator and transporter, which accompanies shipments of hazardous waste to disposal sites.

(D)   The company's proposed plan for safely disposing of hazardous wastes.

147.   Mr. Piglet decides that one way to get easy income is to invite all his friends and neighbors — especially those operating businesses — to dump their garbage on his property, a 500-acre farm in the middle of nowhere. He charges a small fee for each shipment, which he keeps completely confidential to protect the privacy of his customers. A nearby mechanic sends all the used oil, antifreeze, brake fluid, and transmission fluid that he drains from cars, along with dirty grease and other lubricants, to Mr. Piglet's farm. A narrow ravine running through the back of the property makes an ideal place to dump garbage. The county government is delighted because they were already worried about there being little room left in the municipal landfill, and now most of the county's waste is being diverted to My. Piglet's private dump. How does RCRA treat such situations?

(A)   RCRA gives special lenient treatment for private landowners relieving the burdens on local landfills.

(B)   RCRA encourages local governments to seize such properties through eminent domain actions so they can be used as municipal landfills indefinitely.

(C)   RCRA classifies this as a "TSDF" and asks Mr. Piglet to sign "manifests" for all the shipments he receives.

(D)   RCRA classifies this as a "TSDF" and has stringent requirements for obtaining a permit to operate this type of dump.

148.   What are the four chemical characteristics that can qualify a substance as "hazardous waste" under RCRA?

(A)   Lethality, Toxicity, Corrosiveness, and Flammability.

(B)   Toxicity, Corrosiveness, Ignitability, and Reactivity.

(C)   Reactivity, Ignitability, Flammability, and Toxicity.

(D)   Toxicity, Corrosiveness, Reactivity, and Acidity.

149.   A former United States President wants to start a new company, named "Habitat for Humility," that produces tiny, prefabricated igloos (made of plastics) as dwelling structures for humble people who eschew large ostentatious homes. The fabrication of these small plastic igloos will generate hazardous wastes in the process. From the outset, what RCRA requirements demand his attention?

(A)   He needs a permit as a "generator" of hazardous waste, to dutifully prepare manifests for any shipments of waste, and a place to store the waste for up to six months.

(B)   He needs a permit as a "generator" of hazardous waste, plus a "manifest" of all shipments to disposal facilities.

(C)   He needs merely to obtain an EPA I.D. number, prepare manifests for any shipments to disposal facilities, and store the wastes for no longer than three months.

(D)   He needs to obtain an I.D. from the EPA, as well as a permit, and must prepare manifests for all shipments to disposal facilities.

150.   Bob is unemployed but still has his pickup truck, and he decides to make money by hauling away garbage for local businesses. He especially likes to haul away barrels of hazardous wastes because his customers give him a nice "tip" for taking such cargo. What does RCRA require of Bob as a "transporter" of hazardous waste?

(A)   Bob needs to obtain an EPA I.D., must carry manifests of each shipment, and must take the hazardous materials to a permitted TSDF facility.

(B) Bob needs to obtain a permit from the EPA, must carry manifests of each shipment, and must take the hazardous materials to a permitted TSDF facility.

(C) Bob needs to obtain a permit from the EPA, as well as an ID, and must keep manifests of each shipment.

(D) Bob needs to obtain an ID from the EPA, must carry manifests of each shipment, and must take the hazardous materials to an official government disposal site.

151. True or false: liquid sludge can be "solid waste" under RCRA.

(A) True.

(B) False.

152. Which of the following might not be hazardous waste under RCRA?

(A) Specified nuclear or radioactive wastes.

(B) Clear turpentine and similar solvents used to thin paint.

(C) Sand with trace amounts of listed wastes stirred in.

(D) Water from a contaminated well.

153. Peggy likes grilling meat for her family on a charcoal grill, but she is wasteful with the lighter fluid, which contains listed hazardous wastes. In fact, she regularly discards bottles that are still half-full of lighter fluid, throwing them in the trash, which the garbage men take away a few days later. If her ex-husband reports her to the EPA for violations of RCRA, what is the likely result?

(A) Up to $50,000 in fines and five years imprisonment for Peggy.

(B) It depends on whether the container had wasted lighter fluid, under the "contained in rule."

(C) Nothing, because there is a categorical exemption under RCRA for "household wastes" like this.

(D) The EPA will classify her as a hazardous waste generator and demand that she get a permit.

154. Which of the following is a common phrase used to describe RCRA's system for regulating newly-generated hazardous wastes?

(A) "Cradle-to-grave."

(B) "Precautionary Rule."

(C) "*Chevron* Enforcement."

(D)   "Point-source Regulation."

155.   What are three types of "listed" hazardous wastes?

(A)   Solid hazardous waste, liquid hazardous waste, and gaseous hazardous waste.

(B)   Toxic hazardous wastes, Corrosive hazardous wastes, and ignitable hazardous wastes.

(C)   X-waste, Y-waste, and Z-waste.

(D)   F-waste, K-waste, and U & P waste.

156.   For "characteristic" hazardous wastes, "reactivity" often means:

(A)   The substance can explode when it comes into contact with water.

(B)   The substance forms a poisonous liquid when it comes into contact with other liquids, such as water.

(C)   The substance reacts with metal surfaces forming rust and perforations that cause containers of hazardous waste to leak.

(D)   The substance catches fire or explodes easily with even a single spark.

157.   For "characteristic" hazardous wastes, "corrosive" wastes are generally those that could:

(A)   Tarnish metal and ruin valuable items, include the country's coinage and therefore our money supply.

(B)   Corrode metal and thereby eat through metal containers containing hazardous wastes, causing leaks into the environment.

(C)   Contaminate wells and make the water corroded and undrinkable.

(D)   Cause fungus and mold spores to grow.

158.   Frankenstein Laboratories, a wholly-owned subsidiary of a major petroleum company, is conducting experiments on new hydrogen-fuel cell technology. They experiment by filling numerous small canisters with various densities of compressed hydrogen gas, sometimes mixing in gasified Frankincense, which makes the hydrogen fuel smell nice as it burns. When one round of experiments concludes, the lab discards several unused canisters that still contain the compressed gas, in a manner violating RCRA solid waste regulations. When the EPA brings and administrative action against Frankenstein Laboratories, the owners claim that the discarded waste is merely contained gas, and could not possible fall under solid waste disposal regulations. Which side is correct?

(A)   The EPA is right, but only because the canisters are solid; the gas is irrelevant.

    (B)   The Laboratory is right, because RCRA only applies to solid wastes, not to contained gases.

    (C)   The EPA is correct, because contained gases constitute "solid waste" under RCRA.

    (D)   The EPA is correct, but only because some compressed gases turn into liquids and solids under pressure, and it is uncertain whether the containers in question fall into that category.

159.   Under the RCRA "land ban," generators may dispose of hazardous wastes on land as long as two requirements are met. The first requirement is that the facility receiving the waste has been granted a "no migration" permit. What is the second requirement?

    (A)   The waste cannot contain a "listed" hazardous substance.

    (B)   The waste has been specially treated to meet the EPA's BDAT requirements.

    (C)   The waste contains no "reactive" substances that could become dangerous if mixed with certain other substances in a landfill.

    (D)   The generator treats the waste so it meets the current industry standard.

160. Gus owns a gasoline filling station, called Gus' Gas. It is strictly a gas station, and does not offer oil changes or any other services or products besides gasoline, cigarettes, gum, and lottery tickets. Gus' gas tanks, located underneath the concrete near the pumps, have started to leak. Will CERCLA apply to Gus' Gas?

   (A) Yes, because there is a "release" of a hazardous substance into the environment.

   (B) Probably not, because CERCLA does not apply unless the gasoline leaches into the water supply.

   (C) Yes, because gasoline filling stations are strictly liable under CERCLA.

   (D) Probably not, because CERCLA exempts most gasoline and petroleum products, as these are regulated under other statutes.

161. How has CERCLA impacted private causes of action (nuisance, personal injury for toxic torts, etc.)?

   (A) CERCLA pre-empts traditional common law causes of action.

   (B) CERCLA has had no effect on these types of lawsuits.

   (C) CERCLA has boosted these traditional causes of action because CERCLA enforcement produces so much incriminating information against defendants, helps identify every possible defendant ahead of time, and yields a scientific assessment of what steps are necessary to protect human health in the future, etc.

   (D) CERCLA had nearly eliminated private common-law nuisance actions from the federal courts, but not from the state courts, resulting in careful forum-shopping by plaintiffs.

162. The law firm Leachy & Runnig, LLP has a large storage room with stacks of old mimeograph paper (similar to carbon paper, widely used before the advent of photocopier machines), large rolls of "thermal" facsimile paper from the 1980s, gallon jugs of white typewriter correction fluid, and asbestos-padded mailing pouches. Assume that these products contain certain hazardous substances. A tornado destroys the firm's office building and releases their stored hazardous substances into the environment. Could Leachy & Runnig face liability under CERCLA?

   (A) Probably not, because CERCLA's "acts of God" exemption would seem to apply.

(B)   Probably not, because these are necessary and useful office products, regardless of the chemicals they contain.

(C)   Probably not, because it was not foreseeable that the hazardous substances would reach the environment.

(D)   Probably not, because law firms and other professional associations have exemption under CERCLA.

163.   Which of the following is NOT one of the categories of those personally liable under CERCLA?

(A)   Owners-operators.

(B)   Transporters.

(C)   Arrangers.

(D)   Consumers.

164.   Bobby's Bank is the mortgage-holder land used by one of its borrowers for a Laundromat. As the mortgagor, the bank holds a claim in the property, and its security interest is recorded on the title. The land now qualifies as a Superfund site due to the constant dumping of highly toxic chemicals there. Due to the property interest the bank owns, will it be liable for cleanup costs under CERCLA?

(A)   No, because the bank did not generate any of the hazardous substances now contaminating the property.

(B)   No, because the bank would qualify for a "lender's exemption" from CERCLA liability, given the facts described here.

(C)   Yes, because CERCLA is a strict liability statute, and every owner — past, present and future — is liable for cleanup costs.

(D)   Yes, because the bank should have refused to lend money to a Laundromat.

165.   Suppose that Bobby's Bank is a very conservative lender and requires periodic submission of the borrower's business plans and records, financial management, production procedures, etc. The bank's managers are very savvy and frequently require the Laundromat to make changes in its business practices or plans in order to reduce the risk of a default on the mortgage. Can the bank escape "owner" liability under CERCLA, given its security interest in the property?

(A)   No, because CERCLA is a strict liability statute, and every owner — past, present and future — is liable for cleanup costs.

(B)   Yes, because the bank would still qualify for a "lender's exemption" from CERCLA liability, given the facts described here.

(C) No, because a lender's involvement in the management and practices of a borrower corporation can make the lender's exemption inapplicable.

(D) Yes, because the bank could not control the borrower's disposal of hazardous wastes.

166. One of the most difficult problems in the area of CERCLA liability and cleanup is:

(A) . . . the fact that CERCLA itself is probably unconstitutional.

(B) . . . municipal liability.

(C) . . . family farmland.

(D) . . . the unfairness of having judgment-proof transporters.

167. Under CERCLA (and its re-enactment as SARA), what is a "TRI?"

ANSWER:

168. Mr. Moron discovers a lovely tract of land outside of town and inquires about buying it, hoping to build a large estate-style home on the little grassy hilltop in the center of the property. He learns from the local tax assessor's office that the property has lain abandoned for years because the property is on the National Priorities List (NPL), which intimidates many prospective buyers. Mr. Moron assumes this is some prestigious designation for the most beautiful available properties in the country, and immediately begins actions to quiet title and acquire the land. What is the National Priorities List (NPL)?

(A) NPL is the EPA's "top ten most wanted" defendants or pollution sites for upcoming enforcement actions under RCRA.

(B) NPL is the list of the most serious uncontrolled and polluted waste sites identified for long-term remedial action under Superfund.

(C) NPL is the EPA's list of the few remaining properties that are still in their pristine condition, that is, virtually untouched by any pollution.

(D) NPL is the EPA's list of properties the government has acquired through civil asset forfeiture that it most wants to unload.

169. Mr. Moron has now learned what the NPL is, and is wondering if there is automatic liability under CERCLA and other statutes for owners of the property.

(A)   Unless Mr. Moron can meet the stringent requirements for the "innocent landowner" exception, he is instantly liable for the full cost of the remediation as soon as he takes title to the property.

(B)   Mr. Moron could be liable for part of the cleanup costs just because he attempted to purchase the property, because "attempts" create a presumption of guilt under CERCLA.

(C)   Inclusion on the NPL does not create automatic liability under CERCLA or require immediate remediation, but it does present a substantial risk of significant liability for any landowner.

(D)   Mr. Moron will not be liable under CERCLA unless he was personally involved in polluting the property as a generator, transporter, or "arranger."

170.   Mr. Moron next finds a property to purchase that is not on the National Priorities List (NPL) — he checks first. He feels relieved that he will not have to worry about CERCLA liability with this property. Is his confidence well-founded?

(A)   No, because the property could be added to the NPL before he closes on the property.

(B)   No, because there are more than 33,000 sites nationwide that present CERCLA liability issues, even though they are not included on the NPL.

(C)   Yes, if he can show he reasonably relied on the NPL listing before buying his property.

(D)   Yes, because any contaminated property not on the National Priorities List will have its cleanup costs covered by the Superfund instead of private individuals.

171.   In order to qualify for the "innocent landowner" exemption under CERCLA rules, the defendant . . .

(A)   . . . needs to have taken reasonable measures to discover contamination before purchasing the land, needs to mitigate as much as possible, and needs to comply subserviently to the EPA's demands and intrusions.

(B)   . . . needs to have been oblivious to the fact that the land was polluted, and oblivious to the potential for liability.

(C)   . . . needs to prove she was unaware of environmental regulations affecting the property, and still cannot understand anything about the law.

(D)   . . . needs to take full responsibility for the cleanup costs.

172.   CERCLA and RCRA both regulate certain hazardous materials, but differ significantly in the applicability at different points in time. What best describes this difference?

(A)   CERCLA is mostly retrospective and RCRA is mostly prospective.

(B)   CERCLA is mostly prospective and RCRA is mostly retrospective.

(C)   CERCLA is prospective while RCRA is both retrospective and prospective.

(D)   RCRA is retrospective while CERCLA is both retrospective and prospective.

173.   Unlike the citizen-suit provisions of other environmental statutes, CERCLA allows a private right of action to seek:

(A)   injunctive relief.

(B)   money damages.

(C)   genuine apologies from corporations that pollute.

(D)   specific performance.

174.   Which statute regulates more substances that polluters might introduce into the environment?

(A)   CAA

(B)   CWA

(C)   CERCLA

(D)   RCRA

175.   While most environmental statutes (CWA, CAA, RCRA, etc.) regulate the actions of individual polluters (and the substances they introduce into the environment), CERCLA instead regulates:

(A)   endangered animals and plants.

(B)   government agencies.

(C)   nuclear power and nuclear wastes.

(D)   places — contaminated sites.

176.   Inspired by a late-night infomercial, Harry Hapless has made millions buying land and reselling it quickly, with "no money down." One of the properties he bought and resold was next door to a mechanic's shop, and the mechanics dumped their used oil and other fluids drained from engines onto the property in question every day. Harry finds himself paying for all the cleanup costs when the EPA brings a CERCLA action, even though he owned the property for only one or two days. He has the option of suing for contribution from the polluters and other owners, but most of them are insolvent. While

this type of joint and several liability seems severe and unfair, there are several policy justifications for this approach. Which of the following is not one of the justifications?

(A)   This policy shifts cleanup cost from the victims (parties inured by the hazardous substances) to the parties responsible for the pollution.

(B)   This policy has a chilling effect on purchasers of land, which helps keep down housing prices and the cost of doing business.

(C)   This policy creates incentives for safer handling and disposal of hazardous substances, forcing business to "internalize" the true costs of operation.

(D)   This policy alleviates the EPA's litigation costs by forcing defendants to locate and implead other responsible parties who have the resources to contribute to the cleanup.

177.   Harry Hapless was merely trying to make easy money speculating in real estate, and claims he is an "innocent landowner" because he was not aware that the property he bought and sold was being used as a site for releases of hazardous wastes. To maintain his innocence, he refuses to compromise at all with the EPA or return phone calls from agency officials regarding his CERCLA responsibilities. Can Harry avail himself of the "innocent landowner" defense?

(A)   Probably yes, because he was buying and selling properties quickly, without ever visiting the site himself or investigating the current condition of the property.

(B)   Probably yes, because as a policy matter the federal government does not target private land speculators, lest this have a chilling effect on property values appreciating over time.

(C)   Probably not, because he did not exercise due diligence in checking for potential liability before he bought the property, and he now refuses to cooperate with the EPA.

(D)   Probably not, because the EPA will be forced to target him as a wealthy land speculator if the other PRP's are insolvent, which is often the case.

178.   Suppose that Harry Hapless learns his lesson, and the next time he tries to "make millions on real estate with no money down," he obtains a written promise from the seller that the "buyer will not be liable for any CERCLA actions brought by the EPA." The letter is signed and notarized. When the EPA sues Harry for remediation costs on this particular property, he produces this written letter in court, explaining that he has a written promise from the seller that the EPA would never sue him. What will be the legal effect?

(A)   The letter is legally irrelevant to any CERCLA-related proceeding.

(B)   The letter will prevent the EPA from proceeding against Harry, and it will focus its recovery action on the seller instead.

(C)   Under the doctrine of Promissory Estoppel, the letter only saves Harry from liability if he can prove that he reasonably relied on it.

(D)   The letter may give Harry a contract claim against the seller, but it is useless against the EPA.

179.   Dumpitt, Inc. has received a phone message from their legal counsel that the EPA has listed the firm as a "PRP" in a CERCLA matter. Dumpitt's management is concerned because they are not sure what this means, and their lawyer rarely returns their phone calls. What is a "PRP," for purposes of CERCLA?

(A)   Pollution Reduction Permittee.

(B)   Potentially Responsible Party.

(C)   Permittee for Resource Protection.

(D)   Private-Right Plaintiff.

180.   The National Contingency Plan (NCP) identifies certain abandoned hazardous waste sites for long-term remediation plans, which cost millions of dollars. What do we call the conglomeration of all these sites?

(A)   The Superfund.

(B)   The Dirty Dozen.

(C)   The Brownfields.

(D)   The National Priorities List (NPL).

181.   Under CERCLA and SARA, what is the "HRS?"

ANSWER:

182.   Grandpa Jones buried hundreds of barrels of heptachlor (a highly toxic substance) on his farm back in the 1960s, long before CERCLA was enacted. He received a handsome sum of fifty dollars from the nearby chemical company for disposing of their waste. In the 1980s, when he could no longer run his farm, he sold the land to a developer. Now in his twilight years, he has received a legal notice informing him that he is a defendant in an action to seek contribution for CERCLA cleanup costs. Grandpa Jones cannot believe that he is liable for violating a law that did not even exist when he buried the pollutants. Does CERCLA have a "grandfathering" clause?

(A)   CERCLA cannot apply retroactively because this would violate the *ex post facto* clause of the U.S. Constitution.

(B)   CERCLA applies only to "releases" of hazardous substances that occur after the law came into effect.

(C)   CERCLA exempts senior citizens who were unaware of the dangers of pollution in previous eras, at least in cases like this.

(D)   CERCLA's liability provisions apply retroactively in cases like this.

183.   Grandpa Jones next asserts that he had no idea what was in the barrels when he buried them on his farm 40 years ago, nor were most people back then aware of how much damage Heptachlor could cause to the environment. He claims, therefore, that he lacked intent or even sufficient foreseeability to constitute negligence under our legal system. Is this an effective defense?

(A)   Yes, because CERCLA contains a requirement that the defendant "knowingly" released hazardous substances into the environment.

(B)   Yes, because CERCLA contains a requirement that the defendant "willfully" released hazardous substances into the environment.

(C)   No, because CERCLA is a strict liability statute and applies to owners regardless of fault, intent, or mental state.

(D)   No, because there is a presumption that "owners" who actually deposit hazardous waste onto their property are aware that this poses dangers to the environment.

184.   Suppose that most of the contamination of Grandpa Jones' old farm was the fault of subsequent owners, who buried fifty times more hazardous waste there as he did. In fact, the barrels Grandpa Jones buried were sturdy and rust-resistant, so that only a tiny amount of Heptachlor has leaked from the corner of one of the containers, and this miniscule amount did not migrate through the soil more than a few millimeters. The lawyer for Grandpa Jones asserts there was no "release" of hazardous substances into the environment from these barrels. Does this defense release Grandpa Jones from liability?

(A)   No, because the definition of "release" under CERCLA is so expansive as to include every conceivable form of discharge, contact, spill, or leakage.

(B)   No, because Grandpa Jones could never prove that the contamination caused by subsequent owners of the property did not originate with his actions.

(C)   Yes, because of the "de minimis" exception under CERCLA.

(D)   Yes, because the toxin did not migrate and reach the groundwater supply.

185.   Finally, assume that the EPA makes a settlement offer for cleanup costs to all the defendants in the case — Grandpa Jones as well as the defendants who contributed much more hazardous waste to the site. All the other defendants jump at the chance to settle with the EPA, but Grandpa Jones vows to fight. He loses at trial and the court orders him to pay all of the cleanup costs. Now Grandpa Jones sues the arrangers, transporters, generators, and subsequent owners for "contribution" under CERCLA. What is the result?

   (A)   The costs will be divided evenly among all the defendants who are still solvent.

   (B)   The costs will be apportioned based on each responsible party's contribution to the problem.

   (C)   The court will void the previous settlements and order all the parties to negotiate a new comprehensive settlement that includes all the relevant parties to the litigation.

   (D)   The other defendants typically have protection from contribution actions because they settled with the EPA, so Grandpa gets nothing.

186.   With the advent of "tasers," CIA directors decide to stop using chloroform to render enemy spies temporarily unconscious. The CIA buries all its remaining canisters of chloroform in a hazardous waste dump that later becomes a Superfund site. A subsequent owner of the property, facing CERCLA cleanup costs, seeks contribution from the federal government for its share in polluting the site. The government's lawyers contend that the United States Government is not a "person" as defined by the relevant sections of CERCLA. Will this defense work?

   (A)   No, because CERCLA's definition of "person" is so expansive that it includes government entities, including the United States government.

   (B)   Yes, because the United States government cannot be liable under a statute enacted by the federal government itself.

   (C)   No, because CERCLA specifically excludes the CIA from the general exemption given to federal government agencies.

   (D)   Yes, because the CIA has its own exemption from the definition of "person" under CERCLA, due to national security concerns.

187.   Joe Dolt has a pickup truck and frequently hauls trash away for homeowners and businesses. One day a paint store has him take away a few dozen unmarked, metal cans and containers. The cans contain a few ounces of old turpentine, acetone, and other solvents. Mr. Dolt takes the containers to his friend's dump, soon to be a Superfund site. How would Mr. Dolt be classified under CERCLA?

   (A)   Dolt is an "owner" under CERCLA, because he owned the truck or "vessel" in which the hazardous substances were carried.

(B)   Dolt is a "transporter" under CERCLA, because he took the cans from the paint store to the site.

(C)   Dolt is an "arranger" under CERCLA, because he arranged for the hazardous wastes to go from his truck into the dump.

(D)   Dolt is a "generator" under CERCLA, because he contributed directly to the amount of hazardous substances in the soil at the site.

188.   Mosquito Corporation produces a specially-formulated, low-toxicity form of DDT for export to tropical countries. During some remodeling of their facilities, subcontractors throw construction debris, including old floor covering and ceiling tiles, into the dumpster that eventually goes to a private landfill. Small amounts of the "nice" DDT are on the flooring and ceiling tiles. Meanwhile, an Endron subsidiary (now defunct) has been sending hundreds of 55-gallon barrels of regular DDT to the same landfill for disposal. The Endron-owned DDT contaminates the entire site, and soil samples always contain this prevalent contaminant, not the specially-formulated Mosquito-DDT. When the EPA swoops in to do a CERCLA cleanup, can Mosquito Corp. be liable, even though they contributed trace amounts of a chemically-distinguishable substance?

(A)   No, because their contribution was so minimal.

(B)   Yes, despite their minimal contribution and the fact that the chemicals are slightly different on the molecular level, they are still liable.

(C)   No, as long as they can distinguish their produce on the molecular level from the DDT found in random soil samples at the site.

(D)   Yes, but only if Mosquito Corp. intentionally disposed of toxic waste there.

189.   Under the facts above, CERCLA would probably classify Mosquito Corp. as which of the following?

(A)   Owner.

(B)   Arranger.

(C)   Transporter.

(D)   Generator.

190.   If the EPA brings a cleanup and recovery action against Burier Corp. as the sole defendant (despite the fact that their contribution to the contamination was far less than others), what percentage of the cleanup costs will Burier bear?

(A)   The CERCLA defendant will pay only its pro-rata share.

(B)   The CERCLA defendant's share will depend on its willfulness in contributing to the pollution.

(C) The CERCLA defendant has joint and several liability, and is therefore liable for 100% of the costs.

(D) The CERCLA defendant has joint liability and is, therefore, liable for costs divided evenly between the number of identifiable potentially responsible parties.

191. CERCLA authorizes two types of "responses" by the EPA to releases of hazardous substances. What are they?

(A) Remediation and repudiation.

(B) Remediation and removal.

(C) Remediation and recovery of cleanup costs.

(D) Remediation and restoration.

192. Profiteers Corp. is a real estate speculation firm that buys risky properties and leverages the risks against each other. The firm purchases a tract of prime real estate in the downtown district of a major city, knowing that the property is badly contaminated with hazardous chemicals. The property, however, is not included on the NPL, nor is it the subject of a "106 Order" from the EPA, so the firm conducts a thorough cleanup operation without ever getting EPA approval, and then seeks to recover its cleanup costs from a host of previous owners, operators, arrangers, and generators. Will Profiteers succeed in these private actions seeking contribution, even though the government never approved the cleanup or had any involvement?

(A) Yes, as long as the cleanup is consistent with the National Contingency Plan (NCP), there is no requirement for prior government approval before seeking to recover costs of a private cleanup.

(B) No, because the National Contingency Plan (NCP) requires prior government approval before seeking to recover costs of a private cleanup.

(C) Yes, because this is essentially a common-law nuisance action.

(D) No, because only the EPA can initiate any CERCLA actions or cleanups; private cleanups are outside the purview of the Act.

193. Commerce Bank lends money to local businesses for buying property, and holds a mortgage to the land, without getting involved in any of the management decisions or operational issues of its borrowers. When one of its borrowers misses several payments on its mortgage, the Bank forecloses on the property and begins taking proper legal steps to sell it at auction. The borrower polluted the property, however, and it is one step away from being on the National Priorities List. Barrels of hazardous liquids on the property are leaking the toxins into the soil every day. Will Commerce Bank be liable

as an "owner," since it took title to the property in a foreclosure action and there is no other owner who can share in the cleanup costs?

(A) Yes, because taking complete ownership through the foreclosure action eliminated the bank's claim to a "lender's exemption" under CERCLA.

(B) Yes, because the bank should have investigated whether its borrower was polluting the property earlier and tried to stop the pollution.

(C) No, because amendments to CERCLA exempt lenders from CERCLA liability even after foreclosure as long as the lender takes certain steps to sell the land.

(D) No, because the bank was unaware of the pollution and cannot interfere in the business operations of its borrowers.

194. Under CERCLA, what is a "Section 106 Order"?

ANSWER:

195. Eden Corporation produces a modest amount of hazardous waste as part of its manufacturing processes, and the managers conscientiously comply will all legal obligations at the time regarding proper disposal of its waste, regardless of the cost. Its disposal site, however, eventually becomes a Superfund site, and Eden is one of the defendant "generators" in a CERCLA 107(a)3 action. In the meantime, regulations have become much more stringent regarding disposal of the hazardous wastes in question. Can Eden's perfect compliance with the laws at the time of disposal constitute a defense against this type of action?

(A) No, generators cannot use compliance with all legal obligations at the time of disposal as a defense to actions under 107(a)3.

(B) Yes, because CERCLA requires a showing of "knowing violations of the law."

(C) Yes, because CERCLA cannot apply retroactively to generators, so legal actions at the time can never become the basis for liability later on.

(D) Yes, because the EPA will eventually indemnify a generator who demonstrates good-faith effort to comply with the law.

196. The use of "Superfund" money to respond to hazardous substance spills and contaminated disposal sites is governed by:

(A) The National Contingency Plan (NCP).

(B) The Office of Management and Budget.

(C)   The Council on Environmental Quality (CEQ).

(D)   The Senate Ways and Means Committee.

197.   Rico is the President of Gehenna Group, LLC. He manages the day-to-day operations of the firm; in fact, most of his employees consider him a micromanaging control freak. Rico authorizes Joe, a warehouse worker, to take their containers of hazardous waste once a month to an isolated location outside of town and leave them there, which is much cheaper than hiring licensed hazardous material handlers to take the canisters to a TSDF. Years later, when the EPA brings a CERCLA action to clean up Gehenna's dump site, can Rico be personally liable for the costs, or would the costs fall only on the corporate entity, Gehenna Group?

(A)   Under the "responsible corporate officer" (RCO) doctrine, Rico is an RCO and faces personal liability for the cleanup costs.

(B)   Under the "responsible corporate office" (RCO) doctrine, Rico cannot face personal liability because the corporation is responsible for the actions of its officer.

(C)   Under the doctrine of "respondeat superior," Rico evades personal liability because his actions were in the course of his employment.

(D)   Under the "fiduciary duty," doctrine, Rico avoids liability because he had a duty to his shareholders to reduce costs.

198.   Once the CERCLA litigation against them commences, Gehenna Group's lawyers desperately try to use the trick they learned from the film "A Civil Action," in which one of the defendants escapes liability for environmental harms by requesting a bifurcated trial where the jury decides the issue of causation first. The movie, however, was about a traditional wrongful death action, not a CERCLA action, and the rules or burdens about proof regarding causation differ somewhat. What approach does CERCLA take to causation?

(A)   CERCLA uses the doctrine of "proximate causation" borrowed from tort law.

(B)   CERCLA uses a very narrow definition of causation because it is a strict-liability statute, with additional evidentiary burdens beyond those required for "proximate causation" in tort law.

(C)   CERCLA uses a very loose, expansive definition of causation because it is a strict-liability statute, with fewer evidentiary burdens beyond those required for "proximate causation" in tort law.

(D)   CERCLA has its own unique approach to causation, called "necessary" causation, which depends heavily on expert testimony from scientists and carries a rebuttable presumption that the scientists are correct.

199.   Suppose now that both Rico and Gehenna Group approach the EPA seeking to settle the claims, instead of spending enormous amounts of money on litigation costs before they even reach the cleanup costs. What is the EPA's likely response?

    (A)   The EPA cannot enter into settlements under CERCLA's strict, no-settle rules.

    (B)   The EPA can settle with corporate defendants, like Gehenna, but not individual defendants, like Rico.

    (C)   The EPA can settle with individual defendants, like Rico, but not corporate defendants, like Gehenna.

    (D)   The EPA is usually willing and eager to settle with as many defendants as possible.

200. While many environmental statutes have provisions that apply to pesticides, what is the primary federal statute regulating the manufacture and use of pesticides?

 (A) RCRA.

 (B) CWA.

 (C) TSCA.

 (D) FIFRA.

201. Which of the following could not considered a "pest" under FIFRA's definition of that term?

 (A) Elephants.

 (B) Marigolds.

 (C) Telemarketers.

 (D) Cats.

202. FIFRA's regulation of pesticides relies almost entirely on which type of regulatory action?

 (A) Negotiated rulemaking.

 (B) Registration and Labeling requirements.

 (C) Licenses for users.

 (D) Technology-based requirements.

203. What is not one of the three primary requirements for "registration" of a pesticide under FIFRA?

 (A) The product is effective at killing the pests it claims to kill.

 (B) The producer complies with the labeling submission requirements.

 (C) The pesticide is not "unreasonably" dangerous to humans.

 (D) The pesticide does not remain in the environment indefinitely.

204. Under FIFRA, which is the more drastic administrative order, a "cancellation" or a "suspension"?

(A)   A cancellation is more severe because it is permanent and irrevocable.

(B)   A suspension is more drastic, because it mandates immediate cessation of all uses of the substance.

(C)   They are essentially the same remedy and are used interchangeably by the agency.

(D)   A cancellation is more drastic, because it involves the imposition of hefty fines on the manufacturer whose registration was cancelled.

205. The crucial words "reasonable" and "unreasonably" in both TSCA and FIFRA set these statutes apart from other major environmental statutes by mandating what type of analysis on the part of the agency?

(A)   Strict liability.

(B)   Tort-style negligence standards, i.e., the duty of care.

(C)   Cost-benefit analysis.

(D)   Zero tolerance for carcinogens.

206. Farmer Brown has a neurotic phobia of bugs, so he sprays tons of concentrated pesticides every single day on every inch of his property. His neighbor, Farmer Thoreau, is a naturalist who believes pesticides are evil and unnatural. The latter wants to bring a citizen suit against Farmer Brown under FIFRA to enjoin his excessive use of pesticides. Will Thoreau succeed?

(A)   No, because there are no citizen suit provisions of FIFRA; he should sue under one of the other environmental statutes instead.

(B)   No, because FIFRA has automatic exemption provisions for agricultural uses.

(C)   Yes, because FIFRA only allows "reasonable" use of pesticides.

(D)   Yes, because FIFRA embodies common-law nuisance claims as they pertain to pesticides from neighboring properties interfering with the plaintiff's quiet enjoyment of his own property.

207. Assume that Farmer Brown's excessive use of a certain pesticide begins to kill all his neighbors. This concentrated use provides evidence not previously available that the substance is unreasonably dangerous to humans, so the EPA cancels the pesticide's registration under FIFRA, which will eventually lead to its complete removal from the market. Farmer Brown commences an administrative appeal and the proceedings drag on for months and then years. During this time, can Farmer Brown keep using the deadly pesticide every day?

(A)   Yes, unless the EPA issues a "suspension" after documenting that there is an "imminent hazard."

(B)   Yes, because the administrative proceedings constitute "informal adjudication" and are not binding until the decision is final.

(C)   No, because FIFRA requires that all uses of a substance cease once the EPA issues a Notice of Cancellation, until the agency's decision is overturned.

(D)   No, because FIFRA requires that use of a substance ceases if it has directly caused the death of a person.

208.   Little Orphan Annie lost her sight, and all color in her eyes, when she accidentally sprayed herself in the eyes with a potent new pesticide called "Strongman." Daddy Warbucks brings suit on her behalf against the pesticide manufacturer in state court, claiming the pesticide's warning labels were negligently inadequate, given the dangerousness of the product. The warning said simply, "Caution: Keep out of the reach of children," and "It is illegal to use this product in a manner inconsistent with this label." These were the warnings that the EPA required the manufacturer to use after its FIFRA registration. The label said nothing about possible blindness or loss of color in the iris. What is the likely result in this case?

(A)   They will prevail because this is a classic personal injury case based on an inherently dangerous product.

(B)   The court will probably dismiss their case, because it is preempted by FIFRA; as a matter of law, no state can require warnings beyond those approved by the EPA for the product under FIFRA.

(C)   They will prevail under the private cause of action provision in the FIFRA statute, which gives citizens a right to sue the manufacturer of a product if the warning labels are inadequate.

(D)   They will lose their case on the merits, because "Keep out of reach of children" is a warning adequate to cover any injuries to a child from the product.

209.   The Toxic Substances Control Act (TSCA) applies to which of the following?

(A)   Pesticides.

(B)   Food additives and preservatives.

(C)   Narcotics that can cause lethal overdoses.

(D)   PCB's.

210.   Oddball scientist Dr. Mork invents a new substance he calls "flibber," which has remarkable properties and a variety of uses. It also reacts violently certain other

substances and corrodes or "eats through" some metals and plastics. Under Sec 4 of TSCA, what is the first thing the EPA might do to regulate this hitherto-unknown substance, which currently exists only in Dr. Mork's laboratory?

(A) The EPA can ban the substance immediately.

(B) The EPA can identify Dr. Mork as a PRP for future CERCLA actions.

(C) The EPA can require testing to determine the substance's effect on health and the environment.

(D) The EPA can seize the substance and its secret formula through an eminent domain action.

211. A group of environmental activists believes that Dr. Mork's new substance "flibber" will cause serious harm to the environment, so they form a nonprofit organization called S.C.R.A.F. (Scared Citizens Refusing to Accept Flibber) and bring a citizen suit under TSCA to enjoin Dr. Monk from producing any more flibber, before the situation gets out of hand. They also seek monetary damages to serve as a deterrent to future violators. How will S.C.R.A.F. fare in court?

(A) Their case will be dismissed, because there is no citizen suit provision under TSCA.

(B) They will succeed in stalling the approval of Dr. Monk's permit to manufacture flibber, but will receive no monetary damages.

(C) Their case will probably lose at trial, because the product is too new, making it difficult to prove that it causes environmental harm.

(D) Their case will be dismissed unless they can show that flibber will ruin and actual site that the plaintiffs have visited in the past and will visit in the future.

212. Dr. Frankenstein develops a new embalming chemical that actually smells nice. It has the potential to revolutionize the funeral home industry. Frankenstein complies with EPA testing requirements under TSCA and submits the data to the Agency, under a claim of confidentiality. What will the EPA do with the information?

(A) The EPA will use it to determine whether additional regulatory actions are necessary under TSCA's other provisions.

(B) The EPA will prepare an Environmental Impact Statement (EIS) about the effects it will have on the environment.

(C) The EPA will use it to issue NPDES permits under the Clean Water Act.

(D) The EPA will publish all the information about the chemical, its production process, marketing plans, etc. in the Federal Register to comply with TSCA's Notice and Comment requirements.

213. Dr. Frankenstein decides to bring his new, lily-fragranced embalming fluid to market. Having satisfied the initial testing requirements under Section 4 of TSCA, what else must he do under TSCA before marketing his revolutionary product?

    (A) He must obtain a permit from the EPA to manufacture it.

    (B) He must satisfy the requirements of NEPA and prepare an Environmental Impact Statement (EIS) regarding the product.

    (C) He must submit a pre-manufacture notice (PMN) to the EPA, preferably including some additional test results about the safety of the product when used for its intended purpose.

    (D) Nothing — he has satisfied the TSCA regulatory requirements once he completes section 4 testing.

214. Cody is a small business owner. He removes tree stumps for a living and keeps all his tools in his truck. Cody notices that customers who use chemicals to enhance root growth for decorative trees have significant mineral deposits around the roots, and he frequently finds dead rodents (moles, voles, and woodchucks) in the ground around partially-chewed roots. Does TSCA require Cody to report his discovery to the EPA?

    (A) Yes, under TSCA's "whistleblower" statute.

    (B) Yes, there are strict reporting requirements for any party with information that would be useful to the EPA regarding toxic substances.

    (C) No, because there is an exemption under TSCA's reporting requirements for small business owners like Cody.

    (D) No, because the EPA must already be aware of the hazards due to the pre-market testing requirements under TSCA.

215. Delmar is a highly-compensated research scientist employed by a major petrochemical company. During experiments to develop new products. Delmar notices that a rival company's existing product produces a deadly toxin if it mixes with everyday aspirin in the bloodstream of laboratory animals. Is Delmar obligated to report his findings to the EPA?

    (A) Yes, under TSCA's "whistleblower" statute.

    (B) Yes, there are reporting requirements for any party with information that would be useful to the EPA regarding toxic substances, except for small businesses.

    (C) No, because there is an exemption under TSCA's reporting requirements for large conglomerate corporations like Delmar's employer.

    (D) No, because the EPA must already be aware of the hazards due to the pre-market testing requirements under TSCA.

216. One of the main challenges in regulating toxic substances is defining a tolerable level of risk. Which level of risk does FIFRA mandate for the EPA?

   (A) FIFRA allows whatever the agency deems reasonable, taking into consideration the economic concerns involved.

   (B) FIFRA requires a zero-tolerance for risks of cancer in humans, which has been a source of much litigation for the EPA.

   (C) FIFRA mandates regulations that cost no more than $7 million per human life saved.

   (D) FIFRA vests complete and full discretion in the EPA to determine what level of risk is appropriate.

217. Discovery, Inc. develops an edible new fungicide. When added as an ingredient to salad dressings, it makes any mushrooms in the salad instantly disappear, without harming or contaminating the rest of the food. Aware of how popular this will be for "mixed" families of mushroom-lovers and mushroom-haters, Discovery invests in the expensive, time-consuming process of registering the amazing new fungicide with the EPA under FIFRA, which includes submission of the formula and all the tests done to prove that it works and is perfectly safe for human consumption. Unfortunately, the registration documents are also available to the public, so Heynze, the nation's leading producer of salad dressings, steals the idea, makes minor improvements on taste, and submits their own registration packet to the EPA, basically including photocopies of Discovery's testing reports along with a few pages of new material. Discovery feels outraged that their trade secrets are in the hands of their competitors, and demands that the EPA keep its submission confidential. Will the EPA agree?

   (A) Yes, because otherwise FIFRA would provide many opportunities for stealing trade secrets and patented formulas.

   (B) Yes, because FIFRA contains provisions requiring the EPA to protect the research secrets for any product with "significant market potential."

   (C) No, Discovery is completely without recourse, which explains why nobody up to now has bothered inventing a way to rid salads of mushrooms after they're on the table.

   (D) No, the information must be public, but under certain circumstances, FIFRA requires later registrants to pay some compensation to the first registrant for use of their data.

PRACTICE FINAL EXAM: QUESTIONS

INSTRUCTIONS: Suggested time for the examination is 2 hours.

218. What legal document must federal agencies generally publish in the Federal Register in order to avoid completing an EIS for a proposed project, under NEPA?

    (A) An Environmental Assessment (EA).

    (B) A Finding of No Significant Impact (FONSI).

    (C) An Environmental Impact Statement (EIS).

    (D) A categorical exclusion.

219. The EPA decides to regulate emissions of carbon dioxide and other greenhouse gases, and announces a new regulation, effective immediately, which requires car manufacturers to reduce carbon dioxide emissions from new automobiles by 25% over the next five years. Car manufacturers believe this is infeasible and bring suit to challenge the new regulation. Under the Administrative Procedures Act (APA), what is the best legal challenge the car manufacturers could bring, assuming the facts described here?

    (A) The EPA's regulation does not include any consideration of feasibility or cost-benefit analysis.

    (B) The EPA neglected to provide a Notice-and-Comment period for the new regulation.

    (C) The new regulation does not comport with the Best Conventional Technology (BCT) requirement for all environmental regulations.

    (D) The EPA failed to provide any specifics about the consequences for violations or the procedures for enforcement.

220. Alice decides to build a paper mill on her land; the noise and stench make life almost unbearable for all her neighbors. When they bring a common law nuisance action against Alice, which of the following must they prove?

    (A) Possessory interest in their land.

    (B) Interference with the quiet enjoyment of their property.

(C)   That the loss of their property values exceeds the gains from her paper mill.

(D)   That they were living there before Alice built the paper mill.

221.   A group of marine biologists bring suit challenging the Navy's sudden increase in submarine activity in a Hawaiian bay that is a natural mating and feeding habitat for dolphins. The biologists claim the activity is harming the dolphins and their habitat. The named plaintiffs in the action visit the location twice a week to observe and record data about the dolphin population, to take photographs, and to provide veterinary care for any injured dolphins. Three of the biologists, working under existing grant money from the government and the Sierra Club, have bought cottages near the bay and live there for six months out of the year. The Navy claims that they lack standing, because they cannot show any personal interest or injury as a result of the submarine activity. Do the biologists have standing?

ANSWER:

222.   Suppose the EPA responds to political pressure and decides to add carbon dioxide to the list of "criteria pollutants" for purposes of NAAQS regulation under the Clean Air Act. The agency follows all the notice-and-comment requirements of the APA, but the administrative record of decision reveals no scientific research or other justification for the decision besides an email from the Administrator stating simply, "White House called, wants CO_2 regulations now." When the affected industries and disaffected activist groups challenge the new regulation in court, how will the court apply the "hard look" doctrine?

(A)   The court will demand detailed documentation of the agency's careful consideration of all the relevant issues and alternatives, lest the regulation seem "arbitrary and capricious."

(B)   The court will demand detailed documentation of the agency's careful consideration of all the relevant issues and alternatives, lest the regulation seem to lack a "rational basis."

(C)   The court will demand detailed documentation of the agency's careful consideration of all the relevant issues and alternatives, under "de novo" review of the agency's decision.

(D)   The court will defer to the agency's interpretation of its statutory mandate under the "Chevron Doctrine."

223.   Which method of regulation was most predominant under the Clean Water Act, at least as it was originally enacted and enforced?

   (A)   "Technology-based" regulation.

   (B)   "Incentives-based" regulation.

   (C)   "Health-based" regulation.

   (D)   "Technology-forcing" regulation.

224.   Congress decides to address the problem of global warming by creating a new administrative agency to mitigate the adverse effects human-induced climate change. The Global Warming Act, therefore, creates the Climate Change Administration, under the direction of the Climate Change Commissioner. By statute, the Commissioner has "full authority and discretion to any promulgate rules and regulations, bring any enforcement actions, and issue any licenses and permits necessary to produce a beneficial result." The statute contains no other powers or limitations. What constitutional defect is the Supreme Court most likely to find with this statute?

   (A)   The statute violates the Interstate Commerce Clause because it does not specify any ways in which climate change might affect interstate commerce.

   (B)   The statute violates the Due Process Clause of the Fourteenth Amendment by failing to provide fair hearing safeguards for citizens who become targets of enforcement actions.

   (C)   The statute lacks "intelligible standards" and violates the Nondelegation Doctrine.

   (D)   The statute is "void for vagueness."

225.   Alice decides to use her property as a commercial golf driving range, charging customers to come hit golf balls off into the distance. Some of her customers, however, are terrible golfers, and hit the balls at an angle so they fly across a contiguous neighbor's property and land on another neighbor's yard beyond that. When the neighbors in question bring an action in trespass to put a stop to the unwanted golf balls, Alice contends that neither she nor any of her customers ever set foot on the plaintiff's properties, and that the plaintiffs were lucky to get all those free golf balls. Does Alice have a good defense?

ANSWER:

226. The Department of Transportation decides, at long last, to extend Interstate 95 from Florida to Puerto Rico by a series of bridges. Under NEPA, what must the Department do before it commences the project?

(A) The Department must prepare an Environmental Impact Statement (EIS), analyzing the affects the proposed project will have on the environment.

(B) The Department must submit an Environmental Impact Statement (EIS) to the EPA to obtain approval for the project.

(C) The Department must prepare an Environmental Assessment (EA), analyzing the affects the proposed project will have on the environment.

(D) The Department must prepare a cost-benefit analysis of the project and submit it to Congress.

227. Under the Clean Water Act, many facilities must obtain a special permit as a "point source." What type of permit applies to point sources?

(A) TSDF permit.

(B) NAAQS permit.

(C) NSPS permit.

(D) NPDES permit.

228. Suppose the EPA decides to regulate the emission of greenhouse gases, like carbon dioxide, through a system of licenses and permits, and it promulgates the new regulations in compliance with all statutory and constitutional requirements. Under the new rules, every stationary source that emits carbon dioxide must obtain a permit (at a cost of $350 per year for low-level emissions, and $1500 per year for high-level emissions). A local charcoal manufacturing plant operates under the low-level permit, but the EPA discovers that they are emitting ten times as much carbon dioxide as any other high-level permit holders. Outraged, agency officials revoke the factory's permit completely, forcing it to cease operations. The plant wants to challenge the revocation in court; what is its best argument?

(A) The EPA neglected to provide a Notice-and-Comment period for the revocation decision.

(B) The decision is "impracticable" or financially infeasible because the company will go out of business if it cannot operate.

(C) The plant really has no legal arguments in its favor, because the EPA clearly has discretion to revoke permits.

(D) The plant can argue that its due process rights were violated when the EPA did not provide any opportunity for a hearing to contest the revocation.

229.   What is the primary legal mechanism by which states participate in fulfilling the goals
       of the Clean Air Act?

       (A)   The Environmental Impact Statement (EIS).

       (B)   The State Implementation Plan (SIP).

       (C)   The Federal Implementation Plan (FIP).

       (D)   The National Pollutant Discharge Elimination System (NPDES).

230.   Suppose the City of New Orleans starts dumping pollution into the Gulf of Mexico, and
       it washes up on the beaches of Galveston, Texas. The state of Texas, recognizing that
       Galveston beaches are one of its major tourist attractions, brings a nuisance action in
       federal court against New Orleans. What is the likely result?

       (A)   The court will apply Texas nuisance law because they are the victims.

       (B)   The court will apply Louisiana nuisance law because they are the tortfeasors.

       (C)   The court will apply federal common law of nuisance, as the action is between two
             government entities.

       (D)   The court will probably dismiss the action as being pre-empted by federal statute.

231.   Briefly, what is the difference between a "listed waste" and a "characteristic waste"
       under RCRA?

ANSWER:

232.   To which type of pollutants do the National Ambient Air Quality Standards pertain?

       (A)   "Criteria Pollutants."

       (B)   "Characteristic Pollutants."

       (C)   "Listed Pollutants."

       (D)   "Non-point Source Pollutants."

233.   Dale Gribble discovers a very effective pesticide made from a toxin derived from
       tobacco leaves, which he manufactures in a suspension of tar. Under TSCA, what
       requirements apply to Gribble's activities?

       (A)   He needs to submit testing and notifications to the EPA.

       (B)   He needs to obtain a permit from the EPA.

(C)   He needs to apply for a suspension with the EPA.

(D)   He needs to obtain an NPDES permit from the EPA.

234.   Which method of regulation was most predominant under the Clean Air Act, at least as it was originally enacted and enforced?

(A)   "Technology-based" regulation.

(B)   "Incentives-based" regulation.

(C)   "Health-based" regulation.

(D)   "Technology-forcing" regulation.

235.   CERCLA's regulations substances that overlap with which of the following environmental statutes?

(A)   Clean Air Act.

(B)   Clean Water Act.

(C)   RCRA.

(D)   All of the above.

236.   What is a typical "non-point source" under the Clean Water Act?

ANSWER:

237.   Pete has a pickup truck and carries loads of solid waste to the dump for small businesses in his community. What requirements does the EPA place on Pete is he wants to transport hazardous wastes?

(A)   Pete must obtain a permit from the EPA, must prepare a manifest for each shipment, and must deliver the hazardous wastes to an authorized "Treatment, Storage, and Disposal Facility."

(B)   Pete must obtain an I.D. from the EPA, must prepare a manifest for each shipment, and must deliver the hazardous wastes to an authorized "Treatment, Storage, and Disposal Facility."

(C)   Pete must obtain an I.D. and a permit from the EPA, and must deliver the hazardous wastes to an authorized "Treatment, Storage, and Disposal Facility."

(D)   Pete must obtain a permit from the EPA, and must have an EPA I.D. during the transport of the materials, and must prepare a manifest for each shipment.

238. Suppose that twenty different businesses dumped toxic wastes in a private landfill over a period of years, and that the land itself had ten different owners during this period. The EPA finds one Potentially Responsible Party (PRP) and brings a recovery action. Other polluters are still solvent and were responsible for more of the contamination. How much of the cleanup will this PRP be liable for?

    (A)   None of the costs.

    (B)   One-tenth of the costs.

    (C)   All of the costs.

    (D)   One-twentieth of the costs.

239. Dale Gribble starts a business manufacturing pesticides. He receives a legal notice from the EPA threatening him with both "cancellation" and "suspension." Which sanction should be more worrisome to Gribble?

    (A)   A suspension is more drastic, because it mandates immediate cessation of all uses of the substance.

    (B)   A cancellation is more drastic, because it involves the imposition of hefty fines on the manufacturer whose registration was cancelled.

    (C)   A cancellation is more severe because it is permanent and irrevocable.

    (D)   They are essentially the same remedy and are used interchangeably by the agency.

240. Save Us From Ourselves (SUFO) is an environmentalist activist group that wants to litigate against some recent decisions by the EPA. SUFO believes the EPA completely defied its statutory mandate to reduce specific types of pollution. The agency contends that it interpreted the relevant statute differently, and acted accordingly. Given that the case is likely to involve "*Chevron*-type analysis," what would be the most strategic way for the plaintiffs to frame their legal argument?

    (A)   The plaintiffs should argue that the statute is clear and unambiguous, in their favor.

    (B)   The plaintiffs should argue that the statute is ambiguous but the agency's interpretation is unreasonable.

    (C)   The plaintiffs should argue that the EPA is less qualified than the judiciary to interpret the law.

    (D)   The plaintiffs should argue that the EPA's interpretation is inconsistent with the legislative history.

241. Suppose the National Labor Relations Board proposes a new regulation that would require all major employers to provide a company car, large enough to seat seven

passengers, to all union organizers and representatives. The NLRB completes an Environmental Impact Statement (EIS) that concludes the proposed regulation will have huge effects on the environment, greatly increasing the number of large, gas-guzzling vehicles on the road. The CEQ objects to the proposed regulation on the grounds that it will harm the environment and contribute to global warming. What is the legal effect of the CEQ's objection?

(A)   The NLRB must enter negotiations with the CEQ to resolve the dispute.

(B)   The CEQ must publish a report in the Federal Register, recording its objection.

(C)   The NLRB cannot proceed with the project unless it satisfies the CEQ's requirements.

(D)   There is no legal significance to the CEQ's objection.

242.   Obfuscation, Inc. wants to avoid the expense of sending their hazardous wastes to an authorized disposal facility, so they stir the waste into tons of inert sand, and they sell the slightly-tainted sand to construction companies for use in mixing concrete. Which type of rule is mostly likely to apply to this practice?

(A)   The contained-in rule.

(B)   The derived-from rule.

(C)   The mix-in rule.

(D)   The "characteristic waste" rule.

243.   Suppose Congress enacts a Global Warming Act that authorization the EPA to "promulgate and enforce any regulations conducive for the reduction of pollutants and emissions that contribute to global climate change." Instead of regulating carbon dioxide emissions, which the legislative history indicates was Congress' intention, the EPA decides instead to focus exclusively on major pollutants in the ocean, like crude oil spills, on the theory that the death of ocean plankton contributes more to global warming than do automobile emissions. When the oil industry challenges the agency's decisions in court, what is the likely result?

ANSWER:

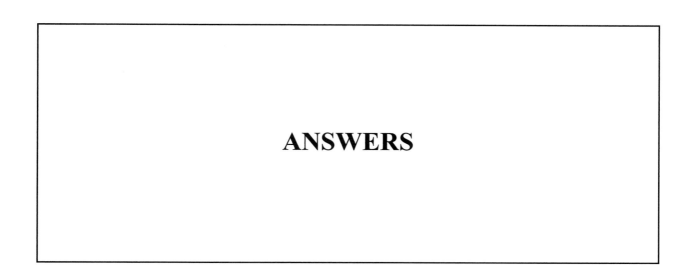

ANSWERS

1. **Answer (B) is correct.** This is a favorite point of emphasis for many professors and textbooks — that modern pollution of water and air, which migrate rapidly across state lines, make localized regulation ineffective. An environmentally-friendly state (from a legal standpoint) that is downwind or downstream from a heavy-polluter state (like the Midwest states with their large power plants) is helpless to stop the deterioration of its air and water quality through its own regulations alone. **Answer (A) is incorrect** because this actually highlights the *problem* with federalized environmental regulation. Consolidation of most of the environmental regulatory power in a single federal agency (the EPA) causes confusing inconsistencies in policies and enforcement every time a new President is elected. **Answer (C) is incorrect** because this is a constitutional clause instead of a policy argument (watch out for this distinction on your exams!). **Answer (D) is incorrect** because the federal regulations themselves do little to force true collaboration between neighboring states, despite the fact that such collaboration would be helpful.

2. **Answer (C) is correct.** The "nondelegation doctrine" is rarely, if ever, used to invalidate a statute, but it operates as an outer limit of Congress' ability to delegate power to administrative agencies like the EPA. Many professors will observe that this doctrine had its heyday long ago in the *Lochner* era, but it was recently discussed at length, and to some extent formally endorsed, in the landmark Supreme Court case *Whitman v. American Trucking.* **Answer (A) is incorrect** because the nondelegation doctrine does not relate to the tension between common law and modern regulatory regimes; the Supreme Court's *Milwaukee II* case addresses this issue. **Answer (B) is incorrect,** because the Executive Branch already has enforcement powers under the U.S. Constitution; the nondelegation doctrine is concerned with the functions of the other two branches, namely rulemaking and adjudication, being turned over to an agency under the control of the Executive Branch, like the EPA. **Answer (D) is incorrect** because the nondelegation doctrine pertains to delegations of authority from one branch of government to another, or from a branch of the government to private individuals, but not to questions of federalism vs. states' rights questions.

3. **Answer (D) is correct.** The courts have held consistently that a statute need merely to provide "intelligible standards," even if they are rather vague and general, to guide the actor (usually an administrative agency) in exercising the delegated authority. Almost anything will suffice, such as "preserve the natural environment." **Answer (A) is incorrect** because the courts do not require details about the parameters of the

delegation at all; there are other safeguards in place, like Congress' ability to amend its statute, its control over budgets, etc. to keep the agency from spinning out of control. **Answer (B) is incorrect** because the courts have held that a statute can have incredibly vague or general expressions of Congressional intent; there is no need for perfect statutory clarity to withstand a challenge under the nondelegation doctrine. **Answer (C) is incorrect** because removal powers are not the issue in nondelegation cases, although removal and appointment powers can become a source of litigation on their own.

4. **Answer (A) is correct.** The courts usually base their nondelegation jurisprudence in the Separation of Powers concept and the "vesting clauses," which "vest" various powers in the three respective branches of government (some professors may call these "enumerated powers" clauses; the terms are used interchangeably). The nondelegation doctrine illustrates the courts' concerns about Congress turning over too much of its authority to an agency, which is usually controlled more directly by the Executive Branch. **Answer (B) is incorrect** because there is no "nondelegation clause" anywhere in the Constitution; like many constitutional doctrines, it is implied by other clauses like the "vesting clauses." **Answer (C) is incorrect** because the Tenth Amendment refers to states' rights, not to transfers of power from Congress to other agencies. **Answer (D) is incorrect** because the Commerce Clause is a justification for Congress to pass laws that apparently interfere with self-government by the states, if the law pertains to a matter than affects interstate commerce (which seemingly includes nearly everything).

5. The common law rules about *nuisance and trespass* were the main ways the legal system addressed environmental concerns, like pollution of water and air, before the modern regulatory system was created. These common law rules were mostly a product of the state courts and varied from state to state; having a unified, *federal* system for protecting the environment supplanted or replaced many of the functions of common law nuisance and trespass.

6. **Answer (C) is correct.** Appleseed lack standing, according to the U.S. Supreme Court. Standing is usually a preliminary matter for the court, and will be grounds for dismissal regardless of the merits of the case itself. There are three primary elements of "standing" for environmental cases: 1) injury in fact; 2) a causal link between the alleged action and the alleged harm to the plaintiff; and 3) legal redressibility of the harm involved. The facts here are reminiscent of two famous Supreme Court cases, *Lujan* and *Sierra Club v. Morton,* both of which involved plaintiffs who could not show how *they* would be harmed by the destruction of the environment in an area far from where they lived. **Answer (A) is incorrect,** because the lawfulness of the logging operations goes directly to the substantive merits of the case, and a court will not reach this issue (or the evidence supporting the argument) if the plaintiff has no standing. If Appleseed *did* have standing, having a permit might be a defense to the action, and the parties would have to litigate about the validity and applicability of the permit. **Answer (B) is incorrect** because cost-benefit analysis like this pertains to the merits of the case (when it applies at all), and the court will never reach such a question if the plaintiff lacks standing. **Answer (D) is**

also incorrect. Regardless of whether Appleseed has evidence to support his claim (the facts here suggest his case is weak), evidentiary matters arise only when the parties reach the trial stage and present their claims; a problem with standing will end the case before a trial occurs.

7. **Answer (D) is correct.** The three traditional requirements for standing are injury in fact (not just a fear of some future injury, or being personally offended at someone's behavior), causation (a tenable connection between the defendant's actions and the harm that came to the plaintiff, and redressibility (the harm is something that a court could avert by ruling on the case). **Answer (A) is incorrect** because these are the equitable requirements for obtaining a preliminary injunction, unrelated to standing. Many students confuse these requirements because most or all of the "standing" cases are about a plaintiff seeking to enjoin activities that are harming or will harm the environment, to these restrictions tend to come up in many of the same cases, even though they relate to a completely separate legal question. **Answer (B) is incorrect** because this echoes the normal level of scrutiny federal courts apply under the Equal Protection clause; it does not relate to standing. **Answer (C) is incorrect** because statutory authorization to bring a type of case (usually referred to as "citizen suit provisions"), does not guarantee that a particular citizen will have standing to bring the suit in question. Most of the "standing" cases in environmental law are also "citizen suits," including the famous cases where plaintiffs were denied standing to bring a claim.

8. **Answer (A) is correct.** Most Environmental Law courses include a few cases on "federal pre-emption," which comes under the Supremacy Clause of the United States Constitution. In most environmental cases, federal law will pre-empt a contradictory state law. The federal law in question may draw its own authority from the Commerce Clause (giving congress the right to regulate anything affecting interstate commerce), but the court's analysis will focus on the Supremacy Clause, and the state rule will usually fail. There are special exceptions for the state of California to make regulations that are more stringent than the EPA's federal regulations, but congress itself acknowledged this exception by statute. **Answer (B) is incorrect,** and this can be a confusing area for students, as many casebooks lump together a few of the Supreme Court's pre-emption cases with some "Dormant Commerce Clause" cases, which *do* base their analysis on the Commerce Clause instead of the Supremacy Clause. The difference is that Supremacy Clause cases involve a state statute, as in the facts described here, which contradicts established federal law. The Commerce Clause usually comes up in environmental cases where there is no federal law at issue, but instead the states are using their own environmental laws for protectionist purposes or to create an economic disadvantage for neighboring states. **Answer (C) is incorrect** for the same reasons described in the previous sentences — most "Dormant Commerce Clause" cases involve no specific federal law. Usually the federal government has not even regulated the area yet, but arguably *could* do so if it wanted — hence the "Dormant"

part of the name. These cases involve state "environmental" regulations that are really thinly-veiled attempts to limit the importation of certain goods from a neighboring state — in other words, to give an advantage to in-state producers under the guise of environmental concerns. **Answer (D) is incorrect** because the state must yield to the federal government if the feds have legitimately regulated an area already.

9. **Answer (C) is correct.** The facts described here are very similar to the famous case *City of Philadelphia v. New Jersey*, where the Supreme Court held that the law was too "protectionist" and encroached upon Congress' exclusive domain to regulate interstate commerce. Note that the cases in this area are fairly unpredictable and confusing; the Supreme Court usually claims to be using the same rule, but seems to produce contradictory results with it from case to case. Even if the outcome is difficult to predict, students should know which constitutional doctrine applies to such cases. There is no existing federal law at stake; we call this *Dormant* Commerce Clause power because Congress has not yet used its constitutional power to regulate this specific issue, even though it *could*. The idea is that the states should leave this to Congress, as it is one of Congress' clearly delineated powers, and when states *do* wander into such areas, it usually creates a conflict between neighboring states. **Answer (A) is incorrect** because the Supremacy Clause will apply only in cases where the state attempts to make a rule that contradicts existing federal law. **Answer (B) is incorrect** because 1) there is no "Nondelegation Clause" in the U.S. Constitution (it is just a judicial doctrine), and 2) there is no delegation issue here in this case. **Answer (D) is incorrect** because the courts will not delegate judicial review of the constitutionality of a statute to the EPA.

10. **Answer (C) is the best answer.** Although courts rarely invalidate agency actions under the Nondelegation Doctrine, when employed it represents a judicial mistrust of agencies, and forces the legislature to take over the governance of that matter instead. **Answer (A) is incorrect** — the *Chevron* Doctrine is the opposite of what is stated in the question, because it is an approach of judicial *deference* to agency action. **Answer (B) is incorrect,** because Dormant Commerce Clause issue arise in the context of state laws or regulations that unfairly affect another state (implying that the matter is best left to the federal government), not to the courts' attitudes towards the administrative agencies themselves. **Answer (D) is incorrect** because federal pre-emption relates to state laws that conflict (or potentially conflict, or are redundant) with federal laws on the same subject; this concept does not pertain to administrative agencies as such.

11. **No, there is no constitutional right to a clean environment,** although some Environmental Law professors may use this as a topic for class discussion or essay exam questions. Of course, many constitutional issues arise in environmental litigation. Free Speech arguments against mandatory reporting requirements are easy to find in the cases. There are Fourth and Fifth Amendment challenges to the rights of EPA agents to inspect polluted properties, or to compel self-incriminating reporting. The Takings Clause arises in "regulatory takings" cases, and Due Process claims are a very common challenge to agency adjudications. Separation of Powers, the Supremacy Clause, and

the case and controversy requirements of Article III are relevant issues to the allocation of authority in environmental rulemaking and enforcement. Nevertheless, repeated pleas for courts to find a constitutional right to a clean environment have failed. Even in a case where a group of Native Americans pleaded for constitutional protection of sacred religious cemeteries, the U.S. Supreme Court declined to find any basis in the U.S. Constitution for preserving the plot of land from development or road construction. *See Lyng v. Northwest Indian Cemetery Protective Ass'n*, 485 U.S. 439, 108 S.Cf. 1319 (1988).

12. **Answer (A) is the best answer.** The scenario described here is very similar to the famous *Vermont Yankee* case, where the Supreme Court upheld the regulatory agency's discretion for determining its own protocol for hearings when making new rules. The APA (Administrative Procedures Act) has hearing requirements for some agency actions. Even so, courts are most likely to apply these requirements to on-the-record adjudication, or in special cases, to agency adjudication generally. In theory, rulemaking applies to the entire population equally, so courts are much less likely to require hearings than for adjudication, which affects the rights of some individual. In *Vermont Yankee*, the agency actually held public hearings about changes in nuclear power plant regulation, but the opponents of nuclear power wanted something more — they wanted to cross-examine high-ranking agency officials instead of the representatives the agency sent to testify and answer questions at the hearings. **Answer (B) is not the best Answer** because "remand without vacatur" is a common procedure courts use when an agency has made technical violations of the APA's requirements for an otherwise valid rule — this allows the agency to go fulfill whatever procedural step it skipped, without starting over again with the promulgation of a new rule. Promulgating new rules is very time-intensive for the agency, and many agencies would give up on making the rule if they had to start over every time there was a minor procedural problem. **Answer (C) contradicts** the Supreme Court's holding in *Vermont Yankee*, a case included in most Administrative Law casebooks. **Answer (D) is incorrect** because the APA has no such exemption for hearing requirements in the type of situation described here.

13. **Answer (C) is the best answer.** The question asked which item is *not* a reason for the EPA to use a licensing and permit scheme instead of command-and-control regulation. The EPA often decides this is the best way to fulfill Congressional intent to limit emissions or new pollution. There are many devices that agencies may use to circumvent control by one of the three branches of government, but this is not one of them. **Answer (A)** is one of the primary benefits of using a licensing or permitting regime, especially in areas where there is uncertainty about the scope of a particular pollution problem, or whether the source of pollution is concentrated (due to a few major polluters who could be regulated more directly). **Answer (B)** is also a good reason for the EPA to use permits, because the self-disclosure by the potential polluters reduces the amount of costly monitoring and surveillance that the agency must do. **Answer (D)** is another common reason for the EPA to use licenses or permits, especially

in situations that are politically controversial, because attaching conditions to permit applications makes compliance seem more voluntary, instead of coerced. Issuing permits to everyone in an industry and attaching conditions for renewal plays on the economic incentives of the regulated parties, and postpones the potential political battle to a future date when the regulated industry will confront the rules individually, instead of collectively (as most parties do not want to litigate to help their competitors get their permits renewed!).

14. **Answer (D) is the best answer.** "Informal adjudication" — like a bureaucrat declining to renew a license or permit — does not require notice-and-comment procedures under the APA. These procedures are for rulemaking, not for adjudication. **Answer (A) is incorrect** because there is no APA violation here, although courts often do invalidated and reverse agency actions when there *is* a violation of the APA. **Answer (B) is incorrect,** but is probably the second-best answer out of the group; sometimes informal adjudication by agencies, including revocation of permits, can infringe on a "property right" of the individual and trigger some procedural due process requirements. In this case, however, declining to renew a permit involves less explicit agency action than revoking a permit before it expires, so there is unlikely to be a "property right" in the expired permit, and hence no due process concerns. **Answer (C) is incorrect** because this is adjudication, not rulemaking.

15. **Answer (A) is the best answer,** because agencies generally have wide prosecutorial discretion — that is, deciding which parties to sue first. Sometimes this is confusing for students, because many Environmental Law casebooks include early CAA cases where courts held that the EPA could not limit its *rulemaking* to certain prioritized pollutants or industries, given the statutory language. Here, we have a case of prosecution and adjudication by the agency, which triggers a different level a review by the courts — more deferential treatment. **Answer (B) is incorrect,** given these facts. A court will find that the agency has wide prosecutorial discretion — but going "outside its statutory authority" is one of the most common grounds for reversal of other agency actions, especially under the "hard look" doctrine. **Answer (C) is incorrect** because the APA's notice-and-comment requirements apply to rulemaking, whereas these facts describe prosecution and adjudication. **Answer (D) is incorrect** but is probably the second-best answer. The presumption, unless otherwise indicated in the statute, is that the EPA has wide prosecutorial discretion, so normally a court would not need to investigate the legislative history to find some implied statutory authority for this discretion. If some language in the statute casts doubt on the agency's authority to select which parties to prosecute first, however, a court would probably look to the legislative history to resolve the question. The facts do not indicate that we have such statutory ambiguity here.

16. **Answer (D) is the correct answer.** Some Environmental Law casebooks spend considerable discussion on overall government policy choices and categories of executive activity, in which case "reg-neg" may feature prominently in the article excerpts in the casebook. **Answer (A) is incorrect** because the phrase "agency capture"

refers to the all-to-common scenario where the President selects insiders from the regulated industry itself to head the relevant agency, based on the presumed expertise of the individuals, so that the agency ends up with leaders who are biased too much in favor of the industry they regulate. **Answer (B) is incorrect** because collective bargaining is a technical term used almost interchangeably for union activity in representing workers in negotiations with their employers. **Answer (C) is incorrect** because this is the (somewhat pejorative) term for traditional bureaucratic rulemaking and enforcement.

17.   **Answer (B) is the best answer**, because normally the Executive (the President) selects agency heads. Appointments are one of the primary ways the Executive Branch controls administrative agencies, as opposed controls by to Congress. **Answer (A) is incorrect** because Congress does exercise great control over agency budgets, and hence, over the agency itself. **Answer (C) is incorrect** because this is the primary way that Congress controls agencies, delegating authority via an enabling statute. **Answer (D) is incorrect** because Congress often overrides agency decisions — especially ones that are politically controversial — by simply passing a statute that renders the offending regulation void.

18.   **Answer (A) is the best answer.** The *Chevron* rule requires courts to give deference to agency interpretations of ambiguous statutes. **Answer (B) is incorrect** because the agency did not exceed the statute as described here, which is very broad. **Answer (C) is incorrect** because Congressional statutes are not under the purview of the APA. This set of facts does not describe the agency promulgating any regulations, just internal policies, and the APA is inapplicable to internal policies of agencies. **Answer (D)** is probably the second-best answer here, because some Congressional statutes are *so vague* or ambiguous that they delegate too much discretion to the agency. The test for such cases is whether the statue includes some "intelligible standards" to guide the agency or define the parameters within which is should operate, and the statute here fits safely within the loose standard most courts use to define "intelligible standards."

19.   **Answer (C) is the correct answer.** This scenario is a classic example of what commentators and scholars call "agency capture." **Answer (A) is incorrect;** "ultra vires" is a Latin phrase for an entity exceeding its legal authority. **Answer (B) is also incorrect,** but is a phrase many students encounter in their Environmental Law casebooks. Justice Cardozo used this epithet to describe an agency action that violates the Nondelegation Doctrine. **Answer (D) is also incorrect;** this is a common phrase used by foreign policy analysts and commentators to describe nations where the Rule of Law is essentially absent from society, and the people feel no connection to their government.

20.   **Answer (B) is the correct answer.** The President of the United States appoints the Administrator of the EPA, as well as Regional Directors. The Appointment Power is the main constitutional control the Executive Branch holds over administrative agencies.

Answer (A) is incorrect, but is probably the second best answer. Executive Order 12,866 (and its progeny) requires administrative agencies to submit a cost-benefit analysis for major proposed regulations to the Office of Management and Budget (OMB), which is closely tied to the White House. The OMB cannot control the budget and salaries completely, but does exert tremendous influence over the agencies. **Answer (C) is incorrect** because the Constitution names the President as Commander-in-Chief of the Armed Forces, not administrative agencies, and the President's authority over agencies cannot compare with the complete control of troop deployments, military divisions, etc. **Answer (D) is incorrect** because normally the President does not initiate regulations, but rather they arise after considerable review and solicitation of public comments by the agency. There may be some instances — especially high-profile matters of public safety, etc. — where the President will ask the agency directly to promulgate certain regulations, but this is the exception, not the rule.

21.   **Answer (D) is correct.** Ronald Reagan's Executive Order 12,866 (and its subsequent revisions) requires administrative agencies to submit a cost-benefit analysis for major proposed regulations to the Office of Management and Budget (OMB), which is closely tied to the White House. The OMB cannot control the budget and salaries completely, but does exert tremendous influence over the agencies. **Answer (A) is incorrect** because the APA itself does not require that regulations be "reasonable" or meet any type of cost-benefit criteria. It is merely a procedural statute. **Answer (B) is the second best answer, but is also incorrect.** The President is unlikely to use this drastic measure, and there are famous cases where the President's removal powers were challenged through litigation. The President probably has the power to fire the EPA Administrator, but would find it politically costly to do so. **Answer (C) is incorrect** because NEPA does not require consideration of economic factors in the Environmental Impact Statement, and the President does not enforce NEPA requirements.

22.   **Answer (A) is the correct answer.** The industry's best argument would be that the EPA does not have authority to restrict fertilizer sales under the authority delegated to it. This is an *ultra vires* act, outside the scope of its delegated power. The connection here between the EPA's action and the verbiage of the statute — which admittedly gives broad discretion to the agency — is too tenuous. **Answer (B) is incorrect,** because courts avoid striking down a statute on constitutional grounds there is another basis for invalidating the agency action, such as the *ultra vires* doctrine. Even if there were a constitutional issue here, it would not be the company's *best* argument to use something that courts consider their *last resort.* **Answer (C) is incorrect;** the agency action described here is not an adjudication or rulemaking. Therefore, the EPA has probably not contravened any procedural requirement from thee APA. (APA § 31-34; 748; 30-33d). **Answer (D) is incorrect,** because under the *Chevron* rule, courts defer to agency interpretations of vague or ambiguous statutes, and this is a very ambiguous statute. Arguing that the agency misinterpreted the statute would not be the best

argument. Even if the agency misinterpreted its authority under the statute, this is not as strong an argument as the *ultra vires* argument.

23. **Answer (B) is the correct answer.** Any action of an agency must fit within its written or implied statutory authority. If an agency acts without such authority, the act is called *ultra vires*. The enabling statute likely does not authorize the agency to allow its facilities to be used in this manner. **Answer (A) is incorrect,** because the notice-and-comment requirements of the APA apply to informal agency rulemaking. The action here is not rulemaking; it is instead an action of particularized applicability. **Answer (C) is incorrect,** because a hearing is required only if a statute or the Constitution requires one. There is no applicable statute that requires a hearing in this problem, nor is there a constitutional right at stake here that invokes due process rights. The constitutional claims made by the Objectivist Society do not relate to agency action against it, but rather unfair privileges being bestowed on another private party. There is no liberty or property interest here to trigger due process rights for the Society. **Answer (D) is also incorrect.** Given that the agency is doing something for which it has no statutory authority, stating a reasonable basis for its decision has no relevance.

24. **Neither the NRDC nor the defendant-polluters are likely to prevail in their arguments.** In general administrative agencies like the EPA have broad prosecutorial discretion. Every agency has a limited budget and must make decisions about how to prioritize cases. Some agencies focus first on cases that present the most potential harm, while others may decide based on the likely costs of the litigation. Political factors also influence agency decisions about prosecution. Students should note that agencies also usually have the authority to decide whether to regulate a certain area primarily through promulgation of rules, or through enforcement actions, which generate a series of case precedents, without making detailed rules first. Historically, the EPA has tended to promulgate detailed rules first, before commencing enforcement actions.

25. **Answer (B) is the correct answer.** Due process requires a hearing before deprivation of property by a governmental entity. Licenses can be "property," once a party obtains the license, meaning the agency must provide a hearing where Hal could rebut the allegations. **Answer (A) is incorrect,** "takings" is a constitutional matter (under the "Takings Clause"), but generally applies to infringement of real property rights by administrative agencies. **Answer (C) is incorrect,** because exercise of enforcement authority by an administrative agency does not violate the "Contracts Clause" of the constitution. **Answer (D) is also incorrect.** As discussed above, Hal could probably obtain a hearing in order to rebut the allegations that he is dumping oil and radiator fluid in the drains.

26. **Answer (B) is the correct answer.** In informal rulemaking, an agency must follow the APA's Notice-and-Comment procedures. This requires both that the agency publish notice of proposed rulemaking in the Federal Register, and that the agency allow a standard period for the public to submit comments before it issues a final rule.

Answer (A) is incorrect. The EPA has a broad grant of authority from Congress to regulate air pollution under the Clean Air Act, so that it can regulate the carbon dioxide emissions from cars without additional permission. **Answer (C) is incorrect,** because the facts do not give any reason to think that the EPA would lack authority to regulate a major category of air pollution. **Answer (D) is incorrect.** As discussed above, the agency has failed to comply with the APA's Notice-and-Comment requirements.

27.   **Answer (D) is the correct answer.** The APA requires agencies to comply with its Notice-and-Comment procedures when engaging in informal rulemaking. **Answer (A) is incorrect;** the APA does not require agencies to consider costs or burdens of regulations, because it focuses only on procedure, not on the content of the rules that agencies promulgate. Other statutes, such as the Regulatory Flexibility Act, may require such considerations. **Answer (B) is incorrect,** because the APA requires hearings for formal on-the-record adjudication or rulemaking, but no necessarily for informal rulemaking, which is the case here. **Answer (C) is incorrect,** because the APA allows agencies to engage in formal and informal adjudication without court approval; in essence, the APA gave took certain functions away from the common law courts and bestowed them on government agencies that Congress can control more easily.

28.   **Answer (A) is the correct answer.** High Courts (such as the U.S. Supreme Court or state Supreme Courts) have retained the sole authority to interpret the Constitution; this is not the domain of administrative agencies. **Answer (B) is incorrect.** The APA provides procedures for formal and informal rulemaking, and agency regulations have the force of law, similar to (but subordinate to) Congressional statutes. **Answer (C) is also incorrect,** because the APA provides procedures for formal and informal adjudication, which sometimes include trial-type hearings similar to an Article III court. **Answer (D) is incorrect.** The APA § 558 provides for the power to issue licenses.

29.   **Answer (C) is the correct answer.** In general, Notice-and-Comment procedures merely require an agency to publish notice of a proposed rule in the Federal Register and to provide a reasonable time for the public to submit comments on the proposed rule. If the final rule is not a logical outgrowth of the proposed rule, the agency is required to provide notice of the revised rule and allow for a comment period. The final rule here is significantly different from the original proposed rule, in that it includes bats. **Answer (A) is incorrect;** as discussed, a rule can be invalid even though the agency complied with Notice-and-Comment procedures if the final rule is not a logical outgrowth of the proposed rule. **Answer (B) is incorrect.** Proposed rules are published in the Federal Register. When the rule becomes final, it appears in the Code of Federal Regulations. **Answer (D) is also incorrect.** Regardless of the agency's discretion to regulate some area, it must still comply with the procedural protocol set forth in the APA, and that is the critical issue here.

30.   **Answer (D) is correct.** The Court in *Citizens to Preserve Overton Park v. Volpe*, 401 U.S. 402 (1971) articulated the arbitrary and capricious test. Under the test, a court can

overturn an agency action if it is done outside the scope of the discretion granted to the agency. The agency must rely upon relevant factors and policies. If the agency fails to articulate a basis for its decision, a court may invalidate it on the basis that it was arbitrary and capricious (or an abuse of discretion). Therefore, a court can inquire into the basis for the action, even though the agency has discretion in the particular area. **Answer (A) is incorrect** because *Overton Park* did not articulate the substantial evidence test. This test relates to a court's ability to overturn an agency's findings if they are unsupported by substantial evidence. **Answer (B) is incorrect** *Overton Park* did not articulate the reasonableness test. This test is a part of the second prong of the *Chevron* test. Under this test, a court will uphold an agency decision if it is a reasonable interpretation of an ambiguous statute. **Answer (C) is incorrect** because *Overton Park* did not articulate the de novo standard of review.

31. **Answer (A) is correct.** The APA says that agency decisions are reviewable unless a statute precludes judicial review. 5 U.S.C. 701. In addition, there is a presumption that agency action is reviewable. *Abbott Laboratories v. Gardner*, 387 U.S. 136 (1967). Therefore, the EPA's argument that Larry must rely on a statute to obtain judicial review is untenable. **Answer (B) is incorrect** because, as discussed, there is a presumption that an agency's action is reviewable. This Answer choice states the opposite. **Answer (C) is incorrect** because the EPA does not need statutory authorization to make this type of motion at trial. **Answer (D) is incorrect** because the facts do not indicate Larry's suit is not yet ripe. A challenge to agency action is ripe if (1) the issues are fit for review and (2) withholding review would create hardship for the parties. It is likely that a court would consider Larry's suit ripe since it involves a final agency action, and withholding review would likely create a hardship for Larry since the decision was adverse to his interests.

32. **Answer (B) is correct.** The Due Process clause and the Takings Clause are likely to form the basis of a challenge to agency action. The Due Process clause requires the government to follow certain procedures if an agency action deprives a person of liberty or property. Discharged government employees or welfare recipients who have their benefits cutoff will often argue that the agency has violated his or her due process rights. The Fifth Amendment Takings Clause will form the basis of a challenge to agency action when the government has "taken" property without providing just compensation. This is often an issue where an agency action causes property to be devalued. **Answer (A) is incorrect** because the Nondelegation Clause is not a likely basis for a challenge to agency action. The Court has consistently upheld broad delegations of authority to agencies. In part, the Court's reluctance to invalidate agency action based on the Nondelegation Clause is its preference to avoid constitutional issues. **Answer (C) is incorrect** because the Contracts Clause is not likely to form the basis of a challenge to agency action. **Answer (D) is incorrect** because the Equal Protection Clause is not likely to form the basis of a challenge to agency action.

33.   **Answer (A) is correct.** The Court has articulated three constitutional requirements: (1) injury-in-fact, (2) causation, and (3) redressibility. *Lujan v. Defenders of Wildlife*, 504 U.S. 555 (1992). **Answer (B) is incorrect** because ripeness and mootness are not constitutional requirements of standings. Ripeness and mootness relate to the timing of judicial review, and whether a court should review the agency action at the particular time. **Answer (C) is incorrect** is incorrect because jurisdiction is not a constitutional requirement for standing. **Answer (D) is incorrect** because domicile and ripeness are not constitutional requirements for standing.

34.   **Answer (A) is correct.** The underlying dispute in *Chevron* was whether the EPA's interpretation of the statutory term "stationary source" was permissible. The EPA interpreted the term "stationary source" to mean an entire factory, rather than one source of pollution in the factory. Consequently, a new source of pollution could be installed in a factory as long as another source of equal or greater pollution was removed. This interpretation is referred to as "the bubble theory." **Answer (B) is incorrect** because the dispute in *Chevron* did not involve estuaries. **Answer (C) is incorrect** because the dispute in *Chevron* did not involve oil and gas regulations. **Answer (D) is incorrect.** The *Chevron* case dealt with the scope of review of agency action, not the Nondelegation doctrine.

35.   **Answer (C) is correct.** The EPA's best argument would be that the industry's suit is not yet ripe. A court must find that a case is ripe for review. The court will consider two factors: (1) fitness of the issues, and (2) hardship to the parties that would result if the court delayed review. In this case, since the regulation has not been specifically applied to anyone, it is likely that a court would say that the issues are not fit for review. Furthermore, it is uncertain that significant hardship would result if the court withheld review. **Answer (A) is incorrect** because a party can challenge agency action even if they are not in the zone of interests that the particular regulation is intended to protect. A party whose interests are adversely affected by an agency action may, in certain circumstances, challenge the validity of the action. **Answer (B) is incorrect** because even if the agency is acting within its statutory authority in making the rule, the rule can still be challenged. The substance of the rule may make the rule invalid (i.e. ultra vires, violation of due process). **Answer (D) is incorrect** because even if the agency complies with the technical requirements of the APA, the rule could still be challenged if it violates other requirements (i.e. constitutional).

36.   **Answer (C) is correct.** The Court in *Chevron* articulated two prongs it will apply in determining whether an agency correctly interpreted a statute. Those prongs are: (1) whether the statute is ambiguous or clear, and (2) if ambiguous, whether the agency's interpretation of the statute is reasonable. If the statute is clear, the agency must give effect to Congress' intent. If the statute is ambiguous, a court will uphold any reasonable interpretation of the statute. **Answer (A) is incorrect** because the *Chevron* case did not articulate these considerations. **Answer (B) is incorrect** because it refers to the APA's Notice-and-Comment requirements. The *Chevron* test does not deal with

Notice-and-Comment. **Answer (D) is incorrect** because it only describes part of the first prong of the *Chevron* test (if Congress' intent is clear, the agency must give effect to it).

37. **Answer (A) is correct.** Among other things, section 706(2)(E) requires that a reviewing court hold unlawful agency findings that are "unsupported by substantial evidence." The requirements apply to actions that require on the record hearings. **Answer (B) is incorrect** because, as discussed, the "substantial evidence" test is applied to actions that require on the record hearings. Informal rulemaking does not require on the record hearings. **Answer (C) is incorrect** because informal adjudication does not require on the record hearings. **Answer (D) is incorrect** because internal agency decisions are generally not subject to the "substantial evidence" test.

38. **Answer (D) is correct.** The APA says that agency actions are reviewable unless a statute precludes judicial review. 5 U.S.C. 701(a)(1). If the court finds that a particular agency action is unreviewable, it will dismiss the challenge regardless of whether it is likely to be meritorious. This is countered by a presumption in favor of judicial review. Therefore, a court will probably be reluctant to dismiss a case for unreviewability unless a statute clearly precludes judicial review. In this case, if the court finds Section 113(h) of the CERCLA statute clearly precludes review it will dismiss the suit. **Answer (A) is incorrect** because the presumption in favor of judicial review is not absolute. As discussed, if a statute precludes review, the presumption is in effect overcome and review will not be available. **Answer (B) is incorrect** because the "hard look doctrine" applies to an agency's exercise of discretion. Here, the agency is not exercising its discretion. Whether judicial review is precluded is a matter of statutory interpretation. **Answer (C) is incorrect.** Whether the challenge is ripe or not may not be important if it is statutorily precluded from review. Assuming a statute does not preclude the challenge, this challenge would probably be ripe. The agency action appears to be a final order and Darrow Corp. would be required to comply.

39. **Answer (B) is correct.** A court will apply the arbitrary and capricious standard when reviewing an agency decision from informal rulemaking. **Answer (A) is incorrect** because the "substantial evidence" generally applies to formal adjudications and rulemaking. **Answer (C) is incorrect** because the arbitrary and capricious standard does not apply to informal adjudication. **Answer (D) is incorrect** because an agency's interpretation of its own rulemaking procedures is entitled to strong deference. This is not the same standard as arbitrary and capricious.

40. **Answer (B) is correct.** The Court in *Chevron* articulated a test that applies to an agency's statutory interpretation. The test applies when an agency engages in various activities (i.e. adjudication or rulemaking). In adjudicating a case or adopting a rule, the agency must interpret the enabling statute to determine whether it has the authority to engage in the particular action. **Answer (A) is incorrect** because *Chevron* does not apply to an agency's decision about whether to use formal or informal rulemaking. Agencies are typically allowed broad discretion in making this decision. **Answer (C) is**

incorrect because *Chevron* does not apply to an agency's decision about whether to use adjudication or rulemaking. A court will usually defer to an agency's decision about whether to use adjudication or rulemaking. **Answer (D) is incorrect** because *Chevron* does not apply to agency rationalizations for its decisions. A court will apply the "substantial evidence" test in determining whether an agency's decision is supported on the record by substantial evidence.

41. **Answer (B) is correct.** This situation is similar to the *Lujan* case. To have standing to challenge an agency action, a plaintiff must (1) suffer a concrete injury-in-fact, (2) show that the action caused the injury, and (3) a favorable ruling would remedy the injury. At issue here is whether the plaintiffs have suffered a sufficiently concrete injury. The injury must be specific to the plaintiffs (not to the general public) and immediate. In this case, where the plaintiffs cannot show that they have seen dolphins or that they plan on traveling to the Pacific Ocean to view dolphins, there is insufficient injury to support standing. **Answer (A) is incorrect.** To have standing, the plaintiffs would have to fall under the zone of interest the statute is intended to protect. **Answer (C) is incorrect** because it implies that a person can assert another's rights. Aside from whether the dolphins would have standing to challenge the agency action, there is a general rule (known as jus tertii) that a person cannot assert the rights of another. **Answer (D) is incorrect** because an organization can have standing to represent the interests of its members. This requires that at least some members of the ground would have standing individually, the interests the organization is trying to protect are germane to its purposes, and the claim does not require the individuals to participate.

42. **Answer (D) is correct.** "Hard look" review calls on the court to ask whether the agency has sufficiently articulated a basis for its decision. Even though courts usually defer to an agency's exercise of discretion, the decision could be found to be arbitrary. For example, if an agency does not respond to comments on a proposed rule, a court might find that the rule is invalid. **Answer (A) is incorrect** because the "de novo" standard of review does not apply to an agency's findings of fact. The standard that will usually apply is the "substantial evidence" standard. **Answer (B) is incorrect.** The "substantial evidence" will usually apply to an agency's findings of fact. This standard, however, is not known as the "hard look" doctrine. The substantial evidence standard is more deferential than the hard look doctrine. **Answer (C) is incorrect** because the "rational basis test" is not the same as "hard look" review. Hard look review asks whether the agency articulated a basis for its decision. This is not the same as the rational basis test, which asks whether the basis the agency articulated is reasonable.

43. **Answer (A) is correct.** The Court in *Vermont Yankee* held, among other things, that courts cannot require procedures in addition to what the APA requires. Inherent in this holding is that an agency should have the discretion to choose which type of rulemaking to use in a given situation. If the agency chooses to use informal rulemaking, a court cannot require that it comply with the requirements of formal rulemaking. **Answer (B) is incorrect** because *Chevron* applies to agency interpretations of statutory language.

Answer (C) is incorrect. While a court will generally defer to an agency's decision about whether to use adjudication or rulemaking, *Vermont Yankee* did not address this type of deference. **Answer (D) is incorrect** because *Vermont Yankee* does not apply to agency rationalizations of its decisions.

44. **Answer (D) is correct.** Hard look review requires a court to ask whether the agency has sufficiently articulated the basis for its decision. If the court finds that it did not articulate a basis, it might find that the decision was arbitrary and capricious. **Answer (A) is incorrect** because an agency's failure to comply with Notice-and-Comment procedures will not render the decision arbitrary and capricious. **Answer (B) is incorrect** because it is not an accurate statement of the "arbitrary and capricious" test. **Answer (C) is incorrect** because the "substantial evidence" test applies to agency findings of fact.

45. **Answer (B) is correct.** Chapter 7 of the APA provides that judicial review is available unless a statute precludes judicial review. 5 U.S.C. 701(a)(1). Therefore, if Clarence does not find a statute that precludes judicial review of agency revocation of permits, he could probably obtain judicial review. **Answer (A) is incorrect** because Chapter 5 of the APA applies to agency procedures, not judicial review in particular. **Answer (C) is incorrect** because the National Environmental Policy Act (NEPA) does not address when judicial review is available. Clarence could not use NEPA as the basis for his challenge. **Answer (D) is incorrect** because the Freedom of Information Act (FOIA) does not provide a basis to review agency action. The Act allows a person to obtain certain documents and information from an agency, but does not provide a vehicle to obtain judicial review of an agency action.

46. **Answer (A) is correct.** The *Chevron* doctrine reflects judicial deference to administrative agencies' interpretations of statutes. When an agency makes a reasonable interpretation of an ambiguous statute, a court will defer to the agency. **Answer (B) is incorrect** because the Dormant Commerce Clause power refers to the implied restriction on states from passing legislation that burdens interstate commerce. This doctrine does not relate to judicial deference to administrative agencies. **Answer (C) is incorrect** because the Nondelegation Doctrine refers to the limitation that courts impose on Congress from delegating too much discretion to agencies. The Doctrine is rarely invoked today but the limitation, theoretically at least, still exists. **Answer (D) is incorrect** because federal preemption refers to the supremacy of federal law over state law.

47. **Answer (D) is correct.** Unlike other sources of nuisance, environmental harms often affect a wide range of people but affect each person only slightly. For example, a factory located near a residential neighborhood could be a nuisance because of its emissions. The harms befalling residents in the general area, however, are often small on the individual level, but large taken together. Each person might think that the nuisance from the emissions are an annoyance, but not worth the time and effort to go through litigation. **Answer (A) is incorrect.** The "race to the bottom" issue exists today. The problem is more likely under a statutory system because a state could change its laws to entice businesses to move there. The problem is less likely under a common law system because *stare decisis* usually implies only incremental changes, and common law judges were relatively immune to corporate-interest lobbyists. **Answer (B) is incorrect.** Enforcement under the common law system was less financially burdensome than it is under the current system. Maintaining the various enforcement agencies is very costly — each must have a full-time staff — whereas the common law system put the burdens on the parties suing, or on defendant polluters who lost their cases. **Answer (C) is incorrect.** This answer sounds funny, but it makes an important point. Under the common law system, a victim had a direct financial interest in bringing a nuisance suit, so a polluter could avoid litigation by simply paying off the plaintiff(s) — i.e., settling the dispute before trial. Regulatory enforcement, by contrast, creates a "whistleblower" problem — a person who complains to a regulatory agency usually has no financial incentive to do so, just a desire to see the law enforced. Violators may have a harder time appeasing the informant than they would have with a common-law plaintiff. For this reason, "whistleblowers" in many arenas are often the victims of unpleasant retaliatory measures or threats.

48. **Answer (B) is correct.** Some activities carry strict liability. That means that if someone engages in such an activity and causes harm, he will be liable for the damages regardless of negligence. One type of activity that carries strict liability is an "ultra-hazardous" or "abnormally dangerous activity." Classifying an activity as "ultra-hazardous" depends on several factors, such as the degree of risk, whether the risk of harm can be eliminated by due care, whether the activity is one of common usage, and whether the activity is appropriate for the place where it is done. Creating sarin, cyanide, and Anthrax clearly presents a risk of harm that could probably not be eliminated with due care. Also, engaging in this activity where contamination to the wells is probably not appropriate. Regardless of whether Professor Frankenstein used excessive care in producing the chemicals, he will probably be liable for the resulting harm. **Answer (A) is incorrect** because, as discussed, even if Professor Frankenstein could negate all allegations of

negligence, he could still be liable for the damages caused by his activities under strict liability. **Answer (C) is incorrect** because whether the Professor has the necessary licenses is irrelevant under strict liability in tort. **Answer (D) is incorrect.** *Res ipsa loquitur* would probably not apply in this situation since there is direct evidence of Professor Frankenstein's conduct.

49. **Answer (C) is correct.** Strict liability means plaintiffs do not have to prove negligence. The plaintiff must still prove causation and damages. Therefore, the plaintiffs in this problem would have to prove that Professor Frankenstein's activities caused the Anthrax poisoning and the contamination of the wells. This poses a problem to plaintiffs in similar situations, because frequently there are several possible causes to environmental harm. It is often difficult to eliminate all other possible causes. **Answer (A) is incorrect** because, as discussed, using the strict liability theory does not relieve the plaintiff of having to prove causation. The tortfeasor's mental state (negligence, intent, etc.) is irrelevant, but causation still matters. **Answer (B) is incorrect** because a plaintiff must still show causation when relying on *res ipsa loquitur*. This negligence theory requires that the plaintiff show the instrumentality that caused the harm was in the defendant's exclusive control. The plaintiff must still show causation. **Answer (D) is incorrect** because the plaintiff bears the burden of proving every element of negligence. If Professor Frankenstein denies that he was negligent, the plaintiffs would have to prove that the Professor's activities caused the harm suffered.

50. **Answer (C) is correct.** There is some indication that common law judges disfavored nuisance plaintiffs, but even if there was a bias, the appellate courts could tweak the common law system by a single ruling, which would be binding precedent on lower-court judges. Judicial bias against plaintiffs was not strong enough to furnish a sufficient reason to abandon the common law system. **Answer (A) is incorrect** because the question asks for a contrary-to-fact answer, and this is an accurate statement. Much of the pollution emitted from factories migrates via the jet stream and becomes difficult to track. The same applies to water as pollution flows downstream, eventually to the banks of another state. **Answer (B) is also incorrect;** this is an accurate statement. Environmental pollution usually is diffuse among the population. Any single person is not likely to suffer enough harm to be motivated to sue. Moving toward a system where the government does the enforcement better protects the aggregate interests of the citizenry. **Answer (D) is incorrect** because, as discussed, several types of pollution travel through the air or water. The result is harm in another jurisdiction, which causes conflicts of law.

51. **Answer (D) is correct.** The plaintiffs here could probably not be successful in a suit now. Merely alleging fear of cancer at a future time is probably not a sufficient injury. Causation and potential damages are not as difficult to prove under these facts as the likelihood of the eventual harm itself. Their injuries are not sufficiently concrete at this point. **Answer (A) is incorrect** because courts generally allow plaintiffs to "plead in the alternative." The plaintiffs here could allege both nuisance and negligence, even if they

are not consistent theories of the case. **Answer (B) is also incorrect.** The main difficulty with proving causation here is that the harms described are still in the future and uncertain. In general, however, a disproportionately high incidence of cancer among the residents exposed to a source of radiation should be sufficient for the jury to infer causation. **Answer (C) is incorrect** because the city has not necessarily rendered the problem moot by changing the source of water. This solution may prevent additional harms, but those already exposed to the radiation can still develop illness or injury that has a remedy at law.

52. **Answer (B) is correct.** The plaintiff cannot bring a claim after he has already litigated the same facts. The doctrine of *res judicata* precludes redundant litigation of a claim in multiple suits. **Answer (A) is incorrect** because plaintiffs cannot recommence the same litigation merely because other potential plaintiffs have emerged. It is true that he would find it easier to prove the same claim now, but that does not help if the litigation is already complete. This is a risk in bringing these toxic-torts suits early. In these types of cases, the first plaintiff has more of an uphill battle than subsequent plaintiffs do. **Answer (C) is incorrect,** although this is the second-best answer. Causation does become harder to prove over time, so if there was new litigation, Rip might face new obstacles in this regard. Even so, the preclusion of his suit is the much more serious problem. **Answer (D) is incorrect** because, as discussed, the issue is not how likely Rip is to be successful on the merits.

53. CERCLA, despite being a strict-liability statute that has many features distinguishing it from common-law claims, has *boosted* common-law personal injury and nuisance claims arising from the same contamination. The main reason for this is the EPA's CERCLA enforcement actions (for which the federal government invests enormous resources) produce an exhaustive amount of useful discovery material for other potential plaintiffs — complete lists of potential (solvent) defendants, information about each defendant's contribution to the contamination, scientific studies about migration of pollutants, causation, chemical similarity of substances, etc. The available of such rich evidence — which would normally be too costly for an individual plaintiff to produce — encourages more plaintiffs to come forward. In addition, CERCLA's joint-and-several liability provisions allow the EPA to impose all the cleanup costs on a single defendant, and then leave it to that defendant to bring private actions for contribution against the remaining defendants — again, leading to more litigation, cross-claims, etc.

54. **Answer (B) is correct.** In order to succeed on a private nuisance claim, the plaintiff must show (1) substantial interference with her use and enjoyment of her land, and (2) that the defendant's conduct was negligent, abnormally dangerous, or intentional. In this case, Sierra Club could not show that the tannery's contamination of the water supply interfered with their use and enjoyment of their land. Unless the Club could show that the tannery's activities affected their land in a way that interfered with their use and enjoyment of it, they would not succeed in a private nuisance action. **Answer (A) is incorrect.** Prospective or future harm cannot provide the basis for a private nuisance

action. The plaintiff is required to show that the defendant has interfered with the use and enjoyment of his land. A predicted interference is not sufficient. Also, a private nuisance claim can be based on aesthetic harm only if it amounts to a substantial interference, consideration being given to the nature of the area. It would be difficult to prove that the tannery's actions substantially interfere with the use and enjoyment of the Club's land based on aesthetic harm. **Answer (C) is incorrect** because the existence of a separate water supply is not necessarily relevant to the tannery's activities. **Answer (D) is incorrect** because even if the tannery's activities have not affected the Club's water, contamination might still exist.

55. **Answer (A) is the correct answer.** The "before-and-after rule" refers to damages where the defendant must restore a polluted property to its original state, to its condition before the nuisance occurred. In certain cases — especially where recent dumping occurred and the pollution has not migrated through the soil or water table yet — this is an especially appropriate remedy. "Special damages" is a rather descriptive term for remedies unique to a particular tort — for example, if a nuisance injured some rare or exotic wildlife on the property, a defendant may need to import replacement specimens to repopulate the fauna of the area, or pay for this repopulation (or reforestation, etc.). Punitive damages are familiar to most law students. Students should be aware that punitive damages can either be retributive (punishing defendants for conduct that is particularly reprehensible or outrageous), or a deterrent (increasing the penalty to offset the low probability of detection or enforcement for certain torts). Injunctions are where a court commands certain behavior — that defendant take certain actions (like removing solid waste dumped on the site), or refrain from certain actions (like ceasing the emission of airborne pollutants). **Answer (B) is incorrect** because executions and evictions were not remedies for common law nuisance actions. **Answer (C) is incorrect,** although these are the main remedies for modern regulatory enforcement. The question asks about nuisance actions. **Answer (D) is incorrect,** although this is the second-best answer here, because it summarizes what inexperienced plaintiffs often want from a case, even if these are not typical legal remedies for tort actions.

56. **Answer (B) is correct.** A public nuisance is an interference with a right common to the public in general. Courts typically apply a balancing test in public nuisances suits, considering the benefits of the activity and the cost it imposes on the public. In this case, a court would consider whether the benefit that the scrap yard provides outweighs the contamination to the surrounding wells. **Answer (A) is incorrect** because public nuisance is not a strict liability offense. As discussed, the court would probably apply a cost-benefit approach, and consider various factors in determining whether the scrap yard is a public nuisance. **Answer (C) is incorrect** because an activity may be a public nuisance even though the entire population does not suffer harm in equal measure. If the harm befalls a small, identifiable group, a court may find that they could just as easily constitute the plaintiffs in a tort action. **Answer (D) is incorrect** because government

officials are typically given the authority to bring a public nuisance claim on behalf of the public.

57. According to some important decisions by the United States Supreme Court, federal statutes have pre-empted the federal common law of nuisance. The leading case in most Environmental Law casebooks is called *Milwaukee II,* which held that the Clean Water Act prevented federal courts from applying federal precedents for nuisance law to contamination of Lake Michigan by the city sewers of Milwaukee.

58. **Answer (B) is correct.** Lawrence could probably be successful in a suit based on the common law doctrine of "Waste." In general, the law of waste allows a landowner to sue a previous owner for permanent harm done to the property. Lawrence could probably recover damages from Morgan for the damage done to his property based on the law of waste. **Answer (A) is incorrect** because the harm that Morgan's landfill is causing is not a harm to the general public. Public nuisance requires an interference with a right common to the larger public. The harm in this case appears to be specific to Lawrence. Unless Lawrence could show that the water running into the storm ditch is a public nuisance, this claim would probably not succeed. Furthermore, it is unlikely that Lawrence would bring a public nuisance action as a private individual. **Answer (C) is incorrect.** A claim based on private nuisance asserts that the defendant's activities are interfering with the plaintiff's quiet enjoyment of his land. This would not be helpful to Lawrence because a favorable result would be an injunction. An injunction would not help Lawrence since Morgan's harmful activities are not ongoing. The law of waste, on the other hand, would allow Lawrence to receive damages for the harm that the landfill is doing to his property. **Answer (D) is incorrect** because adverse possession would not be applicable here. Lawrence already owns the property, so he would not have to rely on adverse possession. Furthermore, suing for adverse possession would not be effective in fixing the problem with the landfill.

59. **Answer (D) is correct.** Trespass and nuisance are similar causes of action, but they protect different rights. Trespass is a cause of action that vindicates the plaintiff's exclusive right of possession. A violation of the exclusive right of possession typically occurs with a physical invasion of the plaintiff's land. In contrast, nuisance vindicates a person's right to use and enjoy his land (quiet enjoyment). In a nuisance claim, a plaintiff does not have to show that the defendant interfered with his exclusive right of possession. Elmer Fudd could probably bring both causes of action against his neighbor. The neighbor's entering Elmer's property to retrieve his rabbits would probably constitute trespass (a violation of Elmer's right of exclusive possession). The rabbits' frequent entry onto Elmer's land would probably constitute a nuisance since it probably interferes with his use and enjoyment of his property. **Answers (A), (B), and (C) are incorrect** because, as discussed, trespass protects one's right of exclusive possession of land and nuisance protects one's right to use and enjoy their land.

60.   **Answer (A) is correct.** Trespass is an intentional tort. A suit for trespass requires a proof of intent. Intent to enter is the issue, not necessarily intent to harm. Nuisance, by contrast, does not depend on showing the defendant intended to interfere with the plaintiff's use and enjoyment of his land. **Answer (B) is incorrect** because whether trespass carries a shorter statute of limitations likely depends on the particular jurisdiction, and trespass does not necessarily carry a shorter limitations period. **Answer (C) is incorrect** because, while it is true that the plaintiff must establish that he owns the property at issue, this is not a significant detriment to the cause of action. A plaintiff should be able to prove that he owns the property easily, if he does in fact own it. **Answer (D) is incorrect;** trespass still exists in most jurisdictions.

61.   **Answer (C) is correct.** The legal rules for nuisance use an objective standard, which is easier for plaintiffs to meet (from and evidentiary standpoint) than the subjective proof needed for showing actual intent. The objective nuisance standard asks whether there was a duty of care in this situation (for example, a foreseeable injury that the defendant could have averted with less loss than the loss sustained by the victim). If there was a duty and the defendant breached the duty, the defendant is legally responsible, regardless of subjective intentions or motivation. Proving intent is usually more difficult because it touches on subjective issues of motivation, purpose, exercise of willpower, etc. The success of either claim typically depends on the proof available. **Answer (A) is incorrect** because it trespass usually does not have a longer statute of limitations than nuisance; rather, nuisance is likely to have a longer period when litigation is still possible, because of exceptions like the "discovery of unknown injuries" rule. **Answer (B) is incorrect** because the typical remedy with nuisance actions is an injunction. A remedy for a trespass action will usually be monetary damages, because in most cases the trespass has ended before the litigation begins. It is true that some parties may want an injunction as their primary goal in litigation; but it is more common for litigation to focus on money damages, and the case is more straightforward than where the court must compel a party to behave in a certain manner. **Answer (D) is incorrect** because this would be a clear advantage of bringing a trespass claim, given that the plaintiff in the facts described here would have some evidentiary difficulties pertaining to the scope of damages.

62.   **Answer (D) is correct.** The issue here is mitigated damages or offsets. A defendant could use evidence of some financial benefit for the victim of the tort to reduce the damage award in the case, but not to escape the basic culpability or verdict of nuisance or trespass. **Answer (A) is incorrect,** because trespass usually requires a showing of only nominal damages. Fudd's *recovery* may be lower because of the offsetting benefit, but his underlying *case* will not falter due to this situation. **Answer (B) is incorrect,** although this is probably the second-best answer. Some courts are very policy-oriented, and they scrutinize social costs and benefits in their analysis of the best legal rule. Even so, these courts would not completely subordinate Fudd's rights to his neighbor's, because property rights are so fundamental to a society based on the "rule of law."

Answer (C) is incorrect, because the diminution of his damages undermines the value of his case (and could, in hindsight, make his lawyer unwilling to bring the case), and could make his showing of a "duty of care" under negligence (especially the foreseeability of the harm to the defendant) somewhat more difficult. He would gain some evidentiary benefit from the defendant's implied admission of the act in question, but the value of this admission depends on whether the defendant was denying the action in the first place, and the fact that this assertion offsets the plaintiff's claimed injuries.

63.   **Answer (D) is correct.** A single wrongful invasion onto a person's land can serve as the basis for a trespass action, although the damages recoverable will probably only be nominal. Of course, repeated invasions can serve as the basis for a trespass action as well. **Answer (A) is incorrect** because this accurately states the rule of trespass, whereas the question asked for a contrary-to-fact answer. **Answer (B) is incorrect** because this is also a common element of trespass. The plaintiff must prove that the invasion was the result of an intentional act. **Answer (C) is incorrect** because foreseeability of the invasion of another's possessory interest is indeed an element of modern trespass.

64.   **Answer (C) is correct.** The plaintiff bringing a public nuisance action must be a state official representing the interests of the citizenry (i.e. the attorney general). **Answer (A) is incorrect** for several reasons. First, as discussed, a public official will usually have to sue under a public nuisance theory, rather than a private individual. In addition, cases such as this would be inappropriate for summary judgment. The case involves complicated questions of fact and proof. **Answer (B) is incorrect** because a court would not dismiss the action based on its belief that the plaintiff couldn't prove causation. Dismissal is for failure to state a claim; causation goes to the proof or merits of the case, and is a better subject for either summary judgment or a jury verdict. **Answer (D) is incorrect** because public nuisance actions do not involve strict liability. A court will apply a balancing test when determining whether a certain activity is a public nuisance.

65. **Answer (B) is the correct answer.** The National Environmental Policy Act (NEPA) applies only to government agencies undertaking projects (public works, government facilities, etc.) that will have a significant impact on the environment. It does not apply to private parties or entities like the Red Cross. Sometimes a government agency hires a private contractor or firm for a particular project, in which case NEPA could apply because a government agency is really sponsoring and directing the project. **Answer (A) is incorrect** because the Red Cross is not a government entity and is not under the purview of NEPA — although this *would* be the remedy in many cases where NEPA applied. **Answer (C) is incorrect** also because NEPA does not apply to private entities like the Red Cross, but this is also one of the common remedies for NEPA violations that students find discussed in their Environmental Law casebooks. **Answer (D) is incorrect** because citizens groups do have standing to bring challenges under NEPA — but having standing does not guarantee that the defendant is covered by the statute.

66. **Answer (B) is the correct answer.** Courts would normally hold that extensive plans to mitigate any environmental impact may be sufficient to satisfy the judge-made requirements of an Environmental Assessment (EA). The courts' concern is to make sure the agency adequately considered is issue of potential environmental effects in deciding not to do the Environmental Impact Statement (EIS), which is much more costly and time-consuming. Extensive planning around the environmental concerns shows this type of agency consideration. **Answer (A) is incorrect** because a valid EA, which legitimately reaches a Finding of No Significant Impact (FONSI), means that the agency does not have to complete and EIS. **Answer (C) is incorrect** because there is no intermediate step between an Environmental Assessment (EA), which is mostly a judicially-created requirement, and the Environmental Impact Statement (EIS), required statutorily under NEPA. **Answer (D) is incorrect,** but is probably the second-best answer. Certain military operations and activities are exempt from NEPA, but the Army Corps of Engineers regularly gets involved in projects for other divisions of the federal government, as in this case. The result specified in this answer is correct, but the reason suggested is not correct.

67. **Answer (D) is the correct answer.** Courts regularly require government agencies to include detailed consideration of project alternatives that would have less impact on the environment, especially if such alternatives are widely accepted and feasible. **Answer (A) is incorrect,** but is probably the second-best answer. The facts here specify a radical proposed project for which there are several easily-imagined alternatives. If this were a more routine proposal, then a court would probably side with the

government as long as it showed adequate research (scientific studies, etc.) supporting its conclusions in the EIS. **Answer (B) is incorrect** because NEPA has no such presumption; on the contrary, newfangled approaches are more likely to invite judicial scrutiny about why traditional methods were not considered. **Answer (C) is incorrect** because the Environmental Assessment (EA) is necessary only to justify an agency's decision to sidestep the preparation of an EIS. If an agency has completed an EIS, there is no need to complete an EA.

68. **Answer (A) is correct.** NEPA allows agencies to delineate and promulgate "categorical exclusions" for their regular, routine activities (as opposed to major new projects or undertakings). Otherwise, citizen activist groups would use NEPA to prevent or hinder agencies from carrying out any functions whatsoever. **Answer (B) is incorrect,** because this terminology is more likely to be a feature of the Clean Air Act, not NEPA requirements. **Answer (C) is incorrect,** but is the second-best answer. Congress can, and does, create statutory exclusions or exemptions from NEPA for specific agencies or agency activities. The facts here, however, describe an agency claiming exclusions for itself, rather than asking Congress to enact the exclusions by statute. **Answer (D) is incorrect,** but may have sounded plausible to students not reading the problem carefully. Agencies do us "project scoping" — that is, breaking a major project into enough smaller projects that each one could escape the onerous burdens of NEPA. Courts are aware of this practice, of course, and could force the agency to consider the project as a whole. Even so, the facts here do not describe "scoping" for a specific project, but rather an agency seeking to exclude its regular, day-to-day activities and functions from NEPA.

69. **Answer (B) is correct.** The Supreme Court and other federal courts have held that psychological effects alone, without concomitant physical effects, are not enough to trigger the requirement of an Environmental Impact Statement, or the revision of a completed EIS to include discussion of these effects. **Answer (A) is incorrect,** although this is one of the common remedies courts use when a single type of environmental impact is missing from the EIS. **Answer (C) is incorrect** because once an EIS is done, the need for an Environmental Assessment becomes moot. And EA is needed only to justify the refusal to undertake an EIS in the first place. **Answer (D) is incorrect,** but this is the second-best answer here. CEQ guidelines do mention "social controversy," which in practice might be almost interchangeable with "psychological effects" (presumably, public outcry is either caused by the psychological effects, or in the alternative, sufficient public outcry can instill enough fear and alarm to create psychological effects where none existed). Even so, it is important for litigants to choose their terms and arguments precisely in NEPA litigation. "Social controversy" might fare better than "psychological effects," a phrase which has been the subject of some unfavorable precedent.

70. **Answer (B) is the correct answer.** There has been voluminous litigation over the requirement that federal agencies complete an Environmental Impact Statement,

because this requires expensive scientific studies, drafting, editing, etc. An EIS consumes significant time and financial resources for the agency, so most agencies try to avoid them. On the other hand, the robust citizen enforcement provisions have given activist groups an opportunity to challenge (on the basis of technicalities with the EIS requirements) government projects that the activists find objectionable. **Answer (A) is incorrect** because there is no such requirement in NEPA. NEPA does not prohibit the government from undertaking environmentally-harmful projects; it just requires careful consideration of all the effects before proceeding. **Answer (C) is incorrect** because the CEQ's review of Environmental Impact Statements is not terribly controversial, and the CEQ does not have authority to stop projects of other agencies even if it finds the EIS conclusions objectionable. **Answer (D) is incorrect** because NEPA does not pertain to engendered species. Protection of species is the subject of the Endangered Species Act.

71. **Answer (A) is correct.** The EPA does not have authority to stop other agencies from pursuing environmentally-harmful projects, at least under NEPA. **Answer (B) is incorrect** because there is no reasonableness or cost-benefit analysis requirement under NEPA. **Answer (C) is incorrect,** but might be the second-best answer. Litigation over an EIS could involve conflicting testimony from each party's experts, but the court cannot stop a government project under NEPA if the agency has satisfied the EIS requirements, regardless of how devastating the project may be. **Answer (D) is incorrect** because the group does have standing under NEPA to challenge agency actions to ensure compliance with NEPA's EIS requirements.

72. **Answer (B) is correct.** Some Environmental Law course may not cover such specific (or real-life) information, but it is helpful for students to be able to picture the difference between completing an Environmental Assessment (the length described here, perhaps similar to the memoranda many law students have to prepare for their legal writing class) as opposed to an EIS, which is much, much longer and more costly to produce. **Answers (A), (C), and (D) are simply incorrect estimates of the number** of pages in an EA.

73. **Answer (D) is correct.** If an agency wants to avoid doing an EIS (and many do), they need to reach a "Finding of No Significant Impact" (FONSI) in the Environmental Assessment. **Answer (A) is incorrect** as the technical term, but may indeed be descriptive of what some agencies are doing when they complete an EA. **Answer (B) is incorrect** because it is a conflation of terms from the Administrative Procedures Act, another meta-statute that governs how government agencies may proceed in their functions. **Answer (C) is incorrect** because "scoping" is the term for the practice of breaking a larger plan into smaller, discreet projects that fall short of the "significant impact" threshold that would trigger the EIS requirement.

74. **Answer (C) is correct.** NEPA applies only to actions by agencies of the federal government. Most states, however, have adopted statute similar to NEPA that applies to their state agencies, albeit under another name. **Answer (A) is incorrect** because NEPA

does not apply to activities by states, although NEPA does require an EIS for federal agencies. **Answer (B) is incorrect** for the same reason (NEPA does not apply to states), but federal agencies generally must complete an EA to justify their decision that an EIS is not required. **Answer (D) is incorrect,** although this is the second-best answer. It is true that NEPA does *not* apply, but the reason stated here is the wrong reason; NEPA could apply to the construction of a government office building.

75.   **Answer (C) is correct.** NEPA instated the Council on Environmental Quality, which sets guidelines for the Environmental Impact Statements, and prepares an annual report for the President on the state of the Environment. **Answer (A) is incorrect,** because the Fish and Wildlife Service has no jurisdiction pertaining to NEPA, although it does play a crucial role in listing and de-listing species under the Endangered Species Act. **Answer (B) is incorrect,** because NEPA gave the EPA no authority whatsoever for enforcement of its provisions. **Answer (D) is incorrect;** the Army Corp of Engineers has no functions or role under NEPA although it has a crucial role in defining Wetlands under the Clean Water Act.

76.   **Answer (A) is correct.** Courts have held that NEPA dos not apply to actions by the EPA, because the EPA's enabling statute already requires it to work for the good of the environment in its activities; presumably, the EPA has already done the same work and research that would be required to complete an EIS. In addition, given that nearly everything the EPA does has a significant impact on the environment (hopefully for the better), imposing the same EIS requirements that other agencies face would mean the EPA would need to do an EIS for nearly every undertaking, which would paralyze the agency and render it defunct. **Answers (B) and (C) are both incorrect** for the reason just discussed — that courts have given the EPA an exemption from NEPA. **Answer (D) is incorrect,** although this is the second-best answer. The case would probably be dismissed, but not for this reason. NEPA does allow citizen groups to bring actions to enforce its provisions.

77.   **Answer (B) is correct.** An EIS is hundreds of pages in length, packed with scientific findings and technical discussion. Preparation of an EIS consumes tremendous resources in terms of time and costs (hiring experts, etc.). **Answers (A), (C), and (D) are simply incorrect** increments of scale. The purpose of this question is to make sure students have a grasp of the length and complexity of an EIS, which explains why it is often worthwhile for an agency to litigate over its refusal to prepare an EIS. On the other hand, the length is not *so* great that the agency would prefer to litigate indefinitely (as in **Answer (D)**); at some point, depending on the length and costs of litigation, it would be cheaper for the agency to either concede and prepare the EIS, or forsake the proposed project — both of which occur from time to time.

78.   **Answer (C) is correct.** NEPA does not require federal agencies to include in its EIS any mitigation plans for the harm it intends to cause to the environment though the proposed project. At the same time, it should be remembered that courts may consider the EIS

incomplete if there is not discussion at all of the possibility of mitigation plans and why they are not included. **Answer (A) is incorrect** because NEPA does not compel agencies to refrain from harming the environment or to offset the damage they propose to do; it merely requires a thorough assessment of the likely harms that will result. **Answer (B) is incorrect** for the same reason — NEPA does not require anything of agencies in terms of friendliness to the environment, other than a frank acknowledgment of the consequences of the agency's intended action. **Answer (D) is incorrect** because NEPA imposes no requirements on the EPA itself.

79. **Answer (C) is correct.** One of the most frequently-litigated aspects of NEPA is whether the proposed agency action constitutes a "major" federal action, because this is one of the elements that defines when an EIS must be done. **Answer (A) is incorrect,** because given the facts here, there is no "major" government action and therefore no need to determine whether there will be "significant impact" on the environment, the determination that an Environmental Assessment would undertake. **Answer (B) is incorrect** because NEPA does not require an EIS unless there is a "major" federal action, which is absent here. **Answer (D) is incorrect** because the group *does* have standing to challenge the action under NEPA.

80. **Answer (D) is correct.** Most Environmental Law casebooks include some federal court decisions requiring agencies to do some preliminary research and prepare a written justification for its refusal to prepare an EIS. The Environmental Assessment (EA) typically satisfies this requirement. Most agencies want to avoid completing an EIS because they are so costly and time-consuming. If there were no requirement that agencies justify their refusal to do an EIS, presumably every agency would merely assert that it the EIS requirements did not apply to its proposed projects, without any other justification.

81. **The correct answer is (C).** NEPA is essentially an information-forcing statute. It forces agencies to face the consequences of proposed actions, and also provides more accountability to the public. **Answer (A) is incorrect** because NEPA does not actually proscribe any deleterious activities that one might think we would want to prevent. **Answer (B) is incorrect** because NEPA does not give any authority to the EPA, unlike most other environmental statutes. **Answer (D) is incorrect** because NEPA does not infringe on common law causes of action, although other federal environmental statutes, like the Clean Water Act, do supplant some common law claims.

82. **Answer (D) is correct.** The negative form of the question is critical here, but students should be watchful for this on exams! NEPA does not directly prohibit agencies from harming the environment, although it has indirectly caused some reduction in government projects that harm the environment. **Answer (A) is incorrect,** because many agencies now would rather forego certain major projects rather than invest the resources in preparing an EIS and litigating over its adequacy. Some agencies have even shifted their overall emphasis so that they can avoid projects that trigger NEPA requirements.

Answer (B) is incorrect because NEPA gave a powerful tool to citizen activist groups that want to forestall certain government projects. **Answer (C) is incorrect;** unfortunately, NEPA has created more taxpayer burdens because major government projects now involve the additional cost of preparing a lengthy, complicated EIS, and often litigating over whether the EIS was thorough enough.

83.   **Answer (C) is correct.** One loophole in NEPA is that agencies can sometimes avoid its requirements by limiting the size of a project just enough to avoid the classification of "major federal action," which would trigger the requirement of an EIS. Similarly, agencies can break larger projects into smaller parts and argue that each is an independent project, too small to warrant a burdensome EIS. **Answer (A) is incorrect;** gerrymandering is drawing jigsaw-like voting districts that break up otherwise unified constituencies that favor the underdog political party. **Answer (B) is also incorrect,** although it is the second best answer here. A FONSI is the conclusion that an agency will reach (justifying the refusal to complete an EIS), after it has engaged in project scoping. IF the scheme is successful, each partial project will have its own EA, each concluding with a Finding of No Significant Impact. **Answer (D) is incorrect;** "eutrophication" is the term used for the process by which a body of water (usually fresh water) becomes satiated with algae as a result of pollutants that cause algae to grow out of control — such as the phosphorous found in common laundry detergents.

84.   **Answer (B) is correct.** Congress can create statutory exemptions from NEPA for certain agency actions, and it often does so. **Answer (A) is incorrect;** while agencies often pursue this strategy ("project scoping"), it is not at Congress' behest. **Answer (C) is incorrect.** Congress does exercise some control over agency budgets, but would not lower a budget merely to avoid NEPA requirements. **Answer (D) is also incorrect.** Congress is unlikely to limit standing under NEPA, which would eviscerate of the statute of most of its usefulness; it is more likely to exempt a particular activity from NEPA's requirements, which accomplishes the same goal with less political price.

85.   **Answer (B) is correct.** NEPA applies to projects, not mere ideas or suggestions. Litigation over an agency's failure to comply with NEPA will not commence until the agency actually commences the project itself. **Answer (A) is incorrect,** because this appears to be still in the conceptual stage, although an EA would be the next step if the agency decides to proceed with the idea as a real project. **Answer (C) is incorrect,** not only because the proposal is still too tentative, but also because the court is more likely to first order an EA than an EIS. **Answer (D) is incorrect** — citizens would have standing, if there was in fact a NEPA violation.

86.   **Answer (A) is correct.** If the agency has dutifully completed its EIS, a court is unlikely to force it to redo everything, or to abandon the project as if no EIS had been done. Rather, most courts would allow (compel) the agency to revise the offending portion of the existing EIS. Nevertheless, even this task is burdensome enough that it may prove worthwhile to the agency to litigate over whether it must revise or amend its EIS even

in part. **Answer (B) is incorrect** because the facts here describe "undeniable physical effects." While courts will usually not require an EIS to consider indirect psychological effects in the absence of any physical harm to the environment, where such harm is likely, psychological and social effects can indeed become mandatory subjects for consideration. **Answer (C) is incorrect** because the court will decide on its own authority whether the EIS should be reopened, rather than leaving this decision to agency, whose self-serving conclusion would be completely predictable. **Answer (D) is incorrect** because the court is unlikely to find the FDA categorically exempt from NEPA.

87. **Answer (C) is correct.** Whether psychological and social effects must be considered in an EIS seems to turn on whether there are also concomitant deleterious physical effects predicted to result from the government project. **Answer (A) is incorrect,** but this is because it assumes an erroneous answer to the previous question. **Answer (B) is incorrect** because the opposite is true — courts seem less concerned with indirect social or psychological harms, at least in enforcing NEPA, than they are with concrete, physical damage to the human environment. **Answer (D) is incorrect** because the court will not ask the agency to complete an EA about whether to modify the EIS, because of the agency's strong bias against undertaking such a costly and lengthy process.

88. **Answer (C) is correct.** The EIS will appear in the Federal Register. It is far too lengthy to publish in a newspaper (an EIS is hundreds of pages long), so **Answer (A) is incorrect.** In addition, **Answer (B) is incorrect,** although agencies do divulge a remarkable amount of useful information on their websites, sometimes voluntarily, and sometimes to satisfy the requirements of a statute. **Answer (D) is incorrect;** the Federal Appendix is a reporter that includes otherwise "unpublished" court decisions that the editors at West think are significant for their value as persuasive authority, especially cases of first impression.

89. **Answer (A) is correct.** An EIS may need revision or amending if significant new information comes to light, and sometimes a court may order this. **Answer (B) is incorrect,** because the agency is too biased against the burdensome prospect of reopening an EIS, so ordering it to prepare an EA on the question would be an exercise in futility. **Answer (C) is incorrect** because an EIS is not "final" in such a strong sense — it is always subject to reopening by a court if sufficiently important new information comes to light. **Answer (D) is incorrect,** as in many previous questions, because the citizen groups clearly have standing to bring a challenge for NEPA violations.

90. **Answer (C) is correct.** The Clean Air Act uses the SIP program to implement many of its provisions. Every state must create a SIP that lays out the emissions limitations and method for each National Ambient Air Quality Standards (NAAQS). The state articulates these requirements through its SIP. Once the state creates its SIP, it then submits the SIP to the EPA for approval. If the EPA approves of the plan, the SIP will have the status of federal law. This SIP will remain effective until the state changes it. Then the EPA must approve the changes. Therefore, any changes to an already approved SIP must be made by the state and agreed to by the EPA. **Answer (A) is incorrect** because, as discussed, an approved SIP remains effective until the state changes the plan's elements. At that point, the EPA must approve the changes. **Answer (B) is incorrect** because a SIP remains effective even if the NAAQS are met. The state must continue monitoring pollution levels. **Answer (D) is incorrect** because even if the NAAQS are not met by the statutory deadline, the SIP remains in effect. After the deadline passes, the "non-attaining" state must expedite its efforts to meet the NAAQS.

91. If the EPA finds that the state has not adopted an acceptable SIP, the EPA has some available sanctions that are aimed at ensuring compliance with the CAA. One of the sanctions is a **Federal Implementation Plan (FIP).** The EPA must adopt federal requirements so that the CAA standards are met. This is generally a lose-lose situation: it is very costly and burdensome for the EPA to create a FIP instead of having the state make its own implementation plan, and the state can find itself burdened with a draconian FIP (or at least one that is not very sensitive to the state's internal political and economic issues). Other sanctions the EPA has at its disposal are (1) the ability to prohibit the granting of highway funding, (2) requiring new sources of pollution to reduce emission by a certain level, and (3) requiring the state to revise its SIP so that it meets the CAA requirements.

92. **Answer (A) is correct;** while normally professors do not expect students to remember or cite individual cases in Environmental Law courses, *Chevron* is the leading exception, because an important legal rule takes its name from this case. The *Chevron* facts were about the "bubble rule," although the case is known more for the rule regarding judicial deference that it lays out. The "bubble rule" was the agency's way of working around an impossibly strict statute that governed construction or modification of new "stationary sources" of pollution. (Basically, the definition of "stationary sources" in Section 113(a)(3), as applied to the NSPS requirements of Section 302(j)). The EPA would deem additions or new structures attached to an existing "stationary source" to be part of the same facility. This was a huge advantage for the facility,

because existing facilities were "grandfathered in" under the statute and exempted from the radically stringent requirements imposed on "new sources;" but the bubble rule sort of eviscerated the strict rule because everyone wanting to build a new facility would simply attach it to an existing one to take advantage of the more lenient statutory requirements. **Answer (B) is incorrect** because the bubble rule did not deal with pollution from automobiles; the case focuses on oil refineries, and the statute in general addresses "stationary sources," and automobiles are not a stationary source. **Answer (C) is incorrect,** although this is the second-best answer. The "bubble rule" and stationary source regulations could be relevant for some State Implementation Plans (one could argue, for example, that the very concept of the SIP is similar to using a "bubble" approach to the overall nonattainment zones in each state). Even so, *Chevron* did not discuss the seldom-kept deadlines for adopting a SIP or complying with NAAQS. **Answer (D) is incorrect** because the bubble rule applied to "stationary sources" of pollution, such as factories. The EPA's obligation to identify and regulate "criteria air pollutants" came from a different section of the Clean Air Act and was not an issue in *Chevron*. The *Chevron* decision is one of the few cases in any law school course that students may need to remember by name, because its holding became the controlling rule defining judicial deference to agency interpretations of statutes.

93.   **Answer (D) is the correct answer.** The definition of "stationary sources" in the 1977 Amendments to the Clean Air Act, impose seemingly impossible emissions requirements on new refineries. See CAA Section 113(a)(3), as applied to the NSPS requirements of CAA Section 302(j). Compliance costs are so high that nearly anyone would feel deterred from constructing a new refinery. **Answer (A) is incorrect,** because CERCLA governs sites with existing ground contamination, and does not regulate future activities like the construction of new oil refineries. **Answer (B) is incorrect,** although this may be the second-best answer, because the CWA's provisions could affect refineries to their extent they discharge pollutants into the water (thus becoming a "point source" under the statute), but the requirements are not as stringent as the 1977 Amendments to the CAA, which were the real deterrent to new construction. **Answer (C) is incorrect** because RCRA does not regulate the construction of new facilities, although a refinery that generates hazardous solid wastes on an ongoing basis will have to comply with RCRA's requirements as well. These requirements, however burdensome they may be, are less of a deterrent to new construction than the CAA regulations.

94.   **Answer (B) is correct.** After the EPA began using the bubble rule to work around the stringent 1977 Amendments to the CAA, many refineries were able to update their facilities or add new structure adjacent to the old ones, and have phased out the older, less-efficient structures in favor of the new replacements. The distinction between a "new source" and an "existing source" is very important. Under the bubble rule, a facility will not trigger application of the stricter provisions of the CAA for being a "new source" if a modification does not increase its emissions. So it is possible that a

refinery might have facilities added to it and still not be considered "new" as long as the emissions are not increased. **Answer (A) is incorrect** because the oil industry is extremely profitable and new refineries would allow entrepreneurs to enter the market, and existing market players to expand their enterprise. **Answer (C) is incorrect** because the 1977 Amendments to the CAA imposed significant legal burden on "new stationary sources." **Answer (D) is incorrect,** although there are significant policy concerns about terrorists targeting our refineries, which would have severe short-term consequences for the national economy. The problem with this answer is that our best refineries are mostly built on the same sites as our older, pre-1977 refineries.

95.   **Answer (A) is correct.** Each State Implementation Plan (SIP) is an elaborate collection of documents that could fill a small warehouse. It is never appears in a single, published form; rather, portions or sections of it become a project for a group of workers at the state environmental agency and at the EPA. There is a relatively famous anecdote about an EPA administrator explaining that just the 1979 amendment to the Illinois SIP filled a box to the point where it was too heavy for many workers to lift. He explained, "We couldn't bring the whole SIP. Nobody could read the whole SIP. Nobody even knows what is in one at this point." How many boxes would a SIP fill? The same administrator answered, "They would measure it in truckloads." (See JOHN-MARK STENSVAAG & CRAIG N. OREN, CLEAN AIR ACT LAW & PRACTICE, 14-4 TO 14-5). **Answer (B) is incorrect,** first because the Federal Appendix is reporter for important "unpublished" decisions by federal district and circuit courts, and also because each state's SIP would itself fill a small library, rather than a single volume. **Answer (C) is incorrect,** although this is probably the second-best answer here. Many of the EPA's decisions related to implementation plans may be published in the Federal Register, as required by the Administrative Procedures Act, but no edition of the Federal Register could hold a SIP (each edition is a paperback book, typically with less than 500 pages). **Answer (D) is incorrect.** Many of the state environmental regulations are indeed posted on state agency websites (not because of the Freedom of Information Act, but rather due to other statutes), and some of these regulations were indeed part of the SIP. The entire SIP, however, is not posted online.

96.   The acronym "SIP" stands for State Implementation Plan. Under the CAA, each state must prepare a plan for attaining compliance to the National Ambient Air Quality Standards, and submit it to the EPA for approval.

97.   **Answer (C) is correct.** The regulated industry is usually the party insisting on cost-benefit analysis as a policy in rulemaking. Where cost-benefit analysis is controlling the regulations, it normally functions as a "cap" on burdensome regulations, forcing the agency to avoid rules that require excessively costly compliance. **Answer (A) is incorrect** because the question asks for a contrary-to-fact answer, and future discounting is, in fact, one of the greatest problems with using cost-benefit analysis in environmental law. Everyone agrees that a million dollars today is worth more than a million dollars at some distant point in the future, but economists and policy analysts

disagree about the best rate to use in calculating the dollar value of future harms and future costs of compliance. Some connect the discount rate to historical inflation rates, while others look at the premium paid on the returns of long-term "locked in" investments. **Answer (B) is also incorrect;** the question asked which one is *not* a problem for cost-benefit analysis, and setting a dollar amount for each human life lost is extremely problematic and complicated. Some commentators prefer to use the current average for wrongful death verdicts (approximately $7 million), which generally correlates to expected earnings over a person's life. Many economists believe a better indicator is the wage premium that workers demand for hazardous jobs, as this indicates the value people are placing on their own lives if they are willing to incur certain levels of risk for some amount of compensation. **Answer (D) is incorrect** because, like valuing a human life, trying to value aesthetic beauty is intangible and subjective, and affixing a dollar value for it is inherently controversial. In addition, many people consider either human life or nature's beauty to have infinite value, which would make cost-benefit analysis impossible.

98.   **Answer (A) is the best argument.** The nature of air pollution necessarily makes it an interstate problem. A factory's pollutants originate in one state, rise into the jet stream, and can be carried north and east across several other states. Pollution sometimes becomes concentrated over some distant region, where it will cause even worse problems, like acid rain. Often it is impossible for the victims to discern where the pollution originated, because it might be hundreds — or thousands — of miles away. Centralized regulation addresses the problem of drifting clouds of contaminants. **Answer (B) is not the best argument.** It is true that states would have contradictory regulations, but this is not the biggest problem. Current variations in state tort laws allow plaintiffs to shop for the best forum in which to bring suit, which is advantageous, at least for plaintiffs. **Answer (C) is not the best answer,** because states already govern themselves in many other areas, but the trend toward a powerful central government continues seemingly unabated. It is a valid argument that each state has the best information and sensitivity to its own pollution problems and manufacturing concerns, so in this sense states are in a superior position to govern themselves in the environmental arena. Even so, this is not as compelling a reason as Answer (A), and the question asked for the "best" argument. **Answer (D) is not the best answer,** even though some states might fail to regulate air pollution, for a variety of reasons, and the citizens there would presumably suffer some health consequences. Offsetting this paternalistic concern is the idea that the residents would either move away to states with healthier environments, or pressure state politicians to act in the public interest.

99.   **Answer (B) is correct.** The Act preempts all states, except California, from establishing their own, stricter, emission limits. The automobile industry, therefore, does not have to design different emissions systems for each state in which it sells cars. A special exception for California allows that state, which has been historically progressive in regulatory measures to preserve the environment, to serve as a laboratory for policies

that are too strict to earn political support on the national level. **Answer (A) is incorrect** because the CAA prevents all states, except California, from enacting stricter regulations than the CAA establishes. **Answer (C) is incorrect** because a state including the regulation in its SIP does not mean that it will be effective. The EPA must approve each state's SIP, and a SIP containing illegal regulations would not obtain approval. **Answer (D) is incorrect** because the mere existence of a federal statute does not automatically preempt state regulations. Congress or the federal courts sometimes allow state rule to continue in parallel to similar federal rules, depending on the nature of the rule and the likelihood of it undermining the goals of federal law. In the case of the CAA, Congress explicitly preempted states from regulating emission limits more strictly than the EPA.

100. **Answer (C) is correct.** The CAA now allows other states to set mobile source emission standards equal to California's stricter standards, but not surpassing the strictness of CA's rules. **Answer (A) is incorrect** because the existence of a federal statute, by itself, does not automatically preempt state regulation. Federal courts consider a variety of factors in preemption cases, including whether Congress explicitly included preemption verbiage in its statute. **Answer (B) is incorrect** because, as discussed, other states can now regulate automobile pollution more strictly, up to the California standards. **Answer (D) is incorrect** because another state does not have to obtain California's permission to enact the same regulations that California establishes.

101. **Answer (A) is correct.** The distinction between the two main types of environmental regulations (technology-based and health-based) is crucial for law students to understand, and is a common issue for testing on exams. Technology-based standards mandate the use of particular emission control devices by the regulated industry. The goal is to reduce overall pollution, of course, but the focus is on the source of new or ongoing pollution, not on removing pollutants that are already released and circulating in the environment. **Answer (B) is incorrect,** as this answer seems to describe typical environmental planning as it applies to zoning and building ordinances. These may be part of the State Implementation Plan under the CAA, but such measures focus on the pollution in a region (the ambient air quality) rather than the emission-control technologies required of certain industries. **Answer (C) is incorrect.** This is a good description of health-based standards, the main alternative to technology-based standards. **Answer (D) is incorrect,** because it does not accurately describe what is normally meant by "technology-based standards." This answer may sound familiar to students, however, because most Environmental Law casebooks include some cases illustrating the complex litigation that arises over which scientific method best determines the "safe" level of some pollutant in the environment, such as lead. This issue is more relevant to health-based standards than technology-based standards.

102. The limitations on the amount of air pollutants that "new or modified stationary sources" can emit are called "New Source Performance Standards" (NSPS), under Clean Air Act Section 111.

103. **Answer (C) is correct,** because this is an accurate, if somewhat simplistic, definition of health-based standards. The important thing for law students is to be able to distinguish health-based standards from technology-based standards, because these two types of regulation are a favorite topic for casebooks, class discussions, and exam questions. **Answer (A) is incorrect,** because this really describes technology-based standards, the main regulatory alternative to health-based standards for regulating emissions of pollutants. **Answer (B) is incorrect,** although health-based standards may lead to the implementation of more stringent emissions controls in certain regions that are outside the safe or healthy levels of pollution (such as "non-attainment zones"). **Answer (D) is incorrect,** because this answer says the regulation covers the technology used to determine healthy levels, which is not the best answer. There has been significant litigation over which scientific method is best for making the determinations of "safe" levels of pollutants (most Environmental Law casebooks have one or two examples of these cases), and the agency may promulgate regulations addressing this issue. Even so, the question of scientific methods or techniques used in this determination is merely a precursor to the actual health-based standard, which mandates that pollution levels in the ambient environment stay below the level determined to be unsafe.

104. **Answer (D) is correct.** The statute requires the EPA to promulgate and enforce NAAQS for each criteria pollutant, which is a very complicated task whose results are guaranteed to be politically controversial and a source of protracted litigation. Consequently, the EPA rarely adds new items to the list of "criteria pollutants." **Answer (A) is incorrect,** because the EPA has authority or discretion to determine safe or acceptable levels of such pollutants in the air, and levels of zero are generally impossible to attain and unnecessary for protecting human health. On the other hand, it is not clear that the EPA can use a cost-benefit analysis or consider economic consequences in determining these levels, so many Environmental Law casebooks have cases that might leave students with the impression that the EPA must adopt the absolute strictest requirements for criteria pollutants (which would logically be a zero-tolerance rule), but that is not accurate. **Answer (B) is incorrect,** because cost-benefit analysis is not part of the EPA's statutory mandate for substances classified as "criteria pollutants," which is part of the reason the EPA is loathe to add any more items to the current list. **Answer (C) is incorrect,** partly because the CAA does not specify special duties for federal agencies with regards to criteria pollutant emissions, and partly because the EIS requirements fall under the purview of NEPA. NEPA does not require an EIS every time a federal agency plans a project that will result in more criteria pollutant emissions; rather, the emissions would have to be enough to constitute a "significant impact on the environment."

105. **Answer (D) is correct,** and students should memorize this short list before their Environmental Law exams. There is, in fact, growing political pressure (and some nascent litigation) to compel the EPA to add carbon dioxide to the list, as it is the main "greenhouse gas" that contributes to global warming. The EPA is averse to adding any more substances to the list and has not done so in many years. **Answer (A) is incorrect,**

as this conflates some terms and definitions from RCRA's classifications for solid hazardous wastes. The "criteria pollutants" are a feature of the Clean Air Act, and refers to suspended airborne substances. **Answer (B) is incorrect,** in that the number is inaccurate (significantly so), but the sources identified are correct. **Answer (C) is incorrect,** because the EPA did manage to include six substances on the list before they stopped adding new ones in the late 1970s. The second part of the statement, however, alludes to a famous case that is included in most Environmental Law casebooks, *NRDC v. Train,* 545 F.2d 320 (2nd Cir. 1976), where the EPA was compelled to add lead to the list of criteria pollutants, despite the agency's well-reasoned decision to use technology-based standards to regulate lead instead.

106.   **Answer (C) is correct.** The National Ambient Air Quality Standards (NAAQS) — which are the maximum levels that the EPA sets for each criteria pollutant — are not directly enforceable. Instead, they become a core feature in the State Implementation Plans. **Answer (A) is incorrect,** because technology-based standards are the primary *alternative* to health-based standards, like the listing of criteria pollutants under the CAA. In at least one case (lead), the EPA would have preferred to reduce emissions through technology-based standards (banning new car engines that run on leaded gasoline), which would certainly have been the most effective route to reducing lead levels in the air, but a court ordered the agency to include lead in the list of criteria pollutants, which triggered a statutory mandate for generating NAAQS for lead. **Answer (B) is incorrect,** because unlike some environmental statutes, the Clean Air Act is a classic example of "command-and-control" regulation, mandating and enforcing compliance with certain standards. **Answer (D) is incorrect,** because the primary enforcement mechanism is indirect, through each state's SIP. There has been, however, an endless stream of litigation from environmental activist groups trying to compel the agency to add additional items to the list of criteria pollutants.

107.   **Answer (B) is correct,** under Sections 171-178 of the Clean Air Act. **Answer (A) is incorrect,** because the "bubble rule" applies to "new stationary sources" and NSPS rules (New Source Performance Standards). There is a sense in which the NAAQS treats each state as its own "bubble" for purposes of making a SIP, but there are special provisions for major urban areas that fail to meet the standards, as in the facts of this question. **Answer (C) is incorrect,** because in most cases the state will include a remediation or control plan for its nonattainment zones in its SIP. A Federal Implementation Plan (FIP) is necessary only where the state fails to submit a SIP that is acceptable to the EPA by its statutory deadlines. Students sometimes become confused about this after reading a famous case, *Delaney v. EPA,* which appears in many Environmental Law casebooks; the *Delaney* case did involve two nonattainment zones in Arizona that triggered a FIP, much to the EPA's chagrin. The basis for that decision, however, was the failure to meet statutory deadlines (and repeated extensions), not the NAAQS violations themselves. **Answer (D) is incorrect,** because it is clear that the EPA has statutory mandate to list criteria pollutants, and to review or revise its list every

five years, under CAA Section 109(d). At the same time, the "arbitrary and capricious" standard is the most common reason for overturning agency decisions under the "hard look" doctrine.

108.   **Answer (A) is correct.** Not since 1978, when the EPA added lead (Pb) to the list under compulsion by a court order, has the agency identified any other criteria pollutants. **Answer (B) is incorrect,** although any changes probably would be published in the Federal Register. The agency can modify or adjust the NAAQS level for each criteria pollutant over time, but it avoids adding any new pollutants to the list. **Answer (C) is incorrect,** because there has been significant public pressure to reduce certain pollutants in the air, such as greenhouse gases that cause global warming. One could argue, perhaps, that there political pressure simply has not been strong enough. **Answer (D) is incorrect,** even though Section 109(d) of the CAA mandates that the EPA revise its list every five years, and various citizen groups have sued repeatedly to compel the agency to do so, courts have held that the EPA must merely consider revising the list, even if it always reaches the same decision to leave the list as it is.

109.   "Smog" is generally a vernacular term for elevated Ozone (O_3) in the air. Other pollutants, such as suspended particulate matter, may reduce visibility or make the city skylines hazy, but Ozone levels are almost interchangeable with "smog."

110.   Sulfur Dioxide (SO_2) is the main culprit for "acid rain." The pollutant enters the atmosphere in large quantities from regional power plants in the Midwestern United States, and often drifts northeast to New England and eastern Canada, where it comes down in the rain. Acid rain erodes buildings and monuments, and poisons ponds, lakes and streams.

111.   **Answer (C) is correct.** In making a State Implementation Plan (SIP) the areas of a state with less pollution need simply retain their current healthy status. BACT regulations are usually less costly and burdensome than those imposed on nonattainment zones. **Answer (A) is incorrect,** because the CAA mandates measures to preserve the air in regions that are not yet polluted. **Answer (B) is incorrect,** because there are special provisions for areas that are particularly unpolluted. "Reasonably Available Control Technology" (RACT) is a feature of the regulations for nonattainment areas, not the pristine areas. **Answer (D) is incorrect,** because "Lowest Achievable Emission Rates" (LAER) is a feature of the regulations for nonattainment areas, not the unpolluted areas described in this problem.

112.   **Answer (D) is correct** (this problem is intended to review the student's grasp of the scope and nature of a SIP, as described in previous answers). A State Implementation Plan (SIP) is an extensive set of rulings, proposals, and research data prepared by each state's own environmental agency as the way to achieve the NAAQS for criteria pollutants. **Answer (A) is incorrect;** a SIP contains tens of thousands of documents in various folders and boxes. **Answer (B) is incorrect;** this describes the approximate size

of the amendments to a single SIP in one calendar year. **Answer (C) is incorrect;** the portion of a SIP relating to one particular item may take up this volume of material.

113. **Answer (A) is correct.** Section 112 of the Clean Air Act requires EPA to promulgate technology-based limits on hazardous air pollutants ("HAPs") for specific groups of industrial sources. These limits are based on "Maximum Achievable Control Technology" ("MACT"). **Answer (B) is incorrect** because health-based standards are the conceptual alternative to technology-based standards, such as MACT requirements. **Answer (C) is incorrect,** because the statutory requirements are explicit, and the MACT requirements are classic command-and-control regulations. The EPA does, however, use protracted negotiation and compromise with regulated industries on other issues. **Answer (D) is incorrect** because RACT rules apply to low-pollution regions that need merely maintain their current, healthful state; the facts here describe a facility emitting HAPs, which triggers the imposition of MACT rules.

114. **Answer (B) is correct.** The EPA regularly uses tradable allowances and offsets to give market-style incentives to reduce pollution emissions. Some Environmental Law professors spend considerable time discussing the auctions, allowances, offsets, and similar economic-based alternatives to the more traditional forms of regulation. The idea with transferable allowances is that unprofitable companies (whose facilities are often the least efficient, meaning they produce more pollution per unit of product or profit than other competitors in the same industry) a financial incentive to stop emitting pollutants. Eventually, the system should consolidate the allowances in the hands of those whose facilities are the most efficient — who produce the least pollution per unit of product or dollar of profit. This, in turn, reduces pollution overall. In addition, the marketability of allowances encourages some firms to hoard them, in hopes of their value increasing, meaning that some allowances will go unused, which is even better for the environment. **Answer (A) is incorrect,** although this could be a criminal penalty for knowing violations of federal environmental laws. **Answer (C) is incorrect** because citizen suits generally target the EPA itself; although some environmental statutes allow citizens to commence enforcement actions against private violators if the relevant agency has failed to do so (these statutory provisions tend to be under-utilized). Here, there is no apparent violation of the Clean Air Act that could furnish the basis for such an action. **Answer (D) is incorrect,** because his decision to cease emissions is probably exactly what the state regulators were hoping for. The allowances or credits he sold may or may not be used immediately by the competitor, so there is a reasonable chance that the aggregate level of emissions will decrease in that region, as well as the ambient air levels of this criteria pollutant. For state regulators trying to cobble together a State Implementation Plan, Cody's cessation gives them more "breathing room" in trying to reduce emissions from the other polluters in that state.

115. **Answer (C) is correct.** This question is intentionally similar to Question 99; the purpose is to help students spot the difference between a CAA question and a CWA question, because law exams frequently have tricky scenarios like this. Unlike the Clean Air Act, the Clean Water Act (CWA) allows states to adopt more stringent regulations than the federal regulations for the same pollutants. **Answer (A) is incorrect,** because this statement describes the Clean Air Act, but does not accurately describe the Clean Water Act. **Answer (B) is incorrect,** because a SIP (State Implementation Plan) pertains to air pollution, especially the NAAQS for criteria air pollutants, not to the CWA. **Answer (D) is incorrect,** because the CWA allows non-conflicting state regulations for water pollutants. Some students may mistakenly choose this answer (or something similar on an exam question), because they are confusing the famous *Milwaukee II* case about federal pre-emption regarding water pollution. That case, however, was about statutory pre-emption of *federal common law of nuisance*, not about state regulations.

116. **Answer (B) is correct.** The study of the Clean Water Act requires some knowledge of certain key vocabulary terms, and "estuary" is a term students are likely to encounter in several cases in their Environmental Law casebooks. **Answer (A) is incorrect;** the more probably term for such mechanisms would be "scrubbers." **Answer (C) is also incorrect,** although nearly all Environmental Law casebooks include opinions by Justice Scalia where he insists on giving statutes their "plain meaning" — usually in siding against the EPA. **Answer (D) is incorrect;** the endangered species in the infamous *TVA v. Hill* case was the "snail darter."

117. **Best Management Practices** is probably the most lenient or permissive standard used in regulating water pollution — basically, common measures already used by responsible companies in a regulated industry for minimizing pollution of nearby waterways. Under CWA Sections 319(a)(1)(C) and 319(b)(2)(A), states must identify the "BMP" wherever state water quality standards are not met due to nonpoint sources. This determines state eligibility for federal technical assistance and program funds. At the same time, these sections create no directly enforceable standards — and in this sense, BMP barely qualifies as a standard at all.

118. **Best Practicable Technology (BPT)** is found in the Clean Water Act in Sections 301(b)(1)(A) & (B), requiring existing sources to meet standards set by "average best performers" in a source category. BPT includes explicit cost-benefit analysis (CBA). This is a standard favored by the regulated industries, because it is favorable to them — the EPA must set the standard at a level where compliance costs are not greater than the supposed benefit of the regulation. In many lists of the continuum of CWA standards,

this will be the most lenient, unless the list also includes BMP (many do not). Students must understand the important difference between the words "practical" and "practicable." The former generally means "effective" or "results-oriented" in environmental statutes or legal writing. The latter means, specifically, *financially affordable*.

119. **Best Conventional Technology (BCT)** in the Clean Water Act appears in Sections 301(b)(2)(E), 301(b)(4)(A), and 301(b)(4)(B), and usually applies to existing sources that cannot meet the stricter "BAT" standard, but produce conventional pollutants (silt, fecal bacteria, etc. — as opposed to highly toxic chemicals). The 1977 CWA Amendments gave existing sources until 1984 to reach the BCT level of compliance. This was supposed to be an intermediate level of strictness between Best Practicable Technology (which means whatever companies can easily afford), and the more demanding Best Available Technology standard, which ignores compliance costs. By "conventional" technology, it generally means whatever is the higher end of the industry standard. BCT includes an explicit requirement of cost-benefit analysis for the agency; the regulations cannot be excessively expensive for the regulated industry. In practice, BCT usually collapses into the BPT standard.

120. **Best Available Technology (BAT)** is more stringent and does not allow the EPA to use cost-benefit analysis in setting specific standards; for some toxins, this may mean that the EPA adopts a zero-tolerance rule (*see* CWA Sec. 307(a)(2)). BAT requirements are present in Sections 301(b)(2)(A) & (B), applying to existing sources (polluters). While BAT does not allow true cost-benefit analysis on the part of the agency, it does allow the agency to set levels that are economically achievable, albeit exorbitantly costly for the regulated industry. The assumption is that the required technology is readily available on the market, but is too expensive for most companies in the industry to use voluntarily. For example, the EPA may require everyone in an industry to match the emissions performance of the single best performer in that category, in terms of pollution reduction. The EPA is required to consider costs, but not to engage in a true cost-benefit analysis (setting the standard low enough that the benefits equaled or outweigh the compliance costs).

121. **Best Demonstrated Available Technology (BDAT)** is the strictest level of regulation short of requiring technology that does not yet exist. Sections 306(a)(1) and (b)(1)(B) of the CWA require this only for new sources (water polluters). This requires the best technology demonstrated (i.e., in a laboratory or at a science fair) available at the time, regardless of its current usage in the market. The EPA must still consider costs (the agency cannot require something that no one in the industry could possibly afford), but the compliance costs can exceed the expected benefits from the regulation. There is no cost-benefit analysis, just a consideration of the maximum cost threshold. In some cases, BDAT can be "technology-forcing," in that it forces companies to find ways to producing an affordable version of some newly-invented technology that has not been brought to market.

122. The answer is *BPT, BCT, BAT, BDAT,* in order of increasing strictness.

123. **Answer (C) is correct.** Any study of the Clean Water Act requires a constant awareness of the place of cost-benefit comparisons, maximum threshold costs, etc. This is a direct result of the CWA's emphasis on *technology-based standards* instead of *health-based standards*. With all the emphasis on requiring specific pollution-control gadgets, the question of how much companies must pay for these required gadgets becomes very relevant. **Answers (A) and (B) are incorrect,** even though they sound plausible, because they are not accurate definitions of the terms. **Answer (D) is incorrect** because it states the opposite of the correct answer.

124. **Best Available Technology (BAT)** is the most common standard under the Clean Water Act for limiting discharges of toxic substances into the waterways.

125. **Answer (A) is correct.** The Clean Water Act is second only to RCRA in furnishing the basis for environmental criminal prosecutions. The penalties are hefty (discussed in later questions). **Answer (B) is incorrect,** perhaps because the extensive industry-agency negotiations that go on in formulating a workable State Implementation Plan; companies are more aware of the requirements and understand that cooperation and compliance. **Answer (C) is incorrect** because NEPA does not have any criminal provisions, and it applies only to federal agencies. **Answer (D) is also incorrect;** RCRA and CWA are the main sources of criminal liability in environmental law.

126. $25,000 per day and one year in prison.

127. **Answer (D) is the correct answer.** Storm water runoff problems are typical of "nonpoint sources" under the CWA, and the business should obtain a permit under the National Pollutant Discharge Elimination System (NPDES), according to Section 401. **Answer (A) is incorrect** because the fact that the trenches are on his property will not prevent the water from migrating eventually to a nearby stream, tributary, or river. **Answer (B) is incorrect,** even though violators often try to use this argument in litigation. The NPDES system — indeed, the entire regulation of "nonpoint sources" — assumes that natural rainfall is the origin of the discharge. **Answer (C) is incorrect,** because NAAQS refers to air pollution standards under the Clean Air Act, not to anything under the CWA.

128. **Answer (A) is the correct answer.** The *Milwaukee II* case is in nearly all Environmental Law casebooks and is a significant milestone in the history of the Clean Water Act. **Answer (B) is incorrect,** because the plaintiffs in the case indisputably had standing to bring the claim. **Answer (C) is incorrect;** even though the Clean Water Act contained numerous deadlines for the EPA to promulgate regulations and for industries to achieve compliance (many of which were missed), there is no "statute of limitations" per se. **Answer (D) is incorrect,** but this refers to another famous case discussed in nearly every Environmental Law survey course, *TVA v. Hill.*

129.   **Answer (B) is the correct answer.** Effluent limitations are part of the technology-based regulatory scheme that pervades the Clean Water Act. **Answer (A) is incorrect,** although this is a recurrent problem with the water environment, and is subject to special regulations, including the common law "right of capture" rules, where applicable. **Answers (C) and (D) are incorrect** because they are inaccurate definitions of "effluent limitations" under the Clean Water Act.

130.   **Answer (A) is correct.** It is very important for students to understand the difference between "technology-based standards" (which comprise the main thrust of the original CWA) and "health-based standards" like those pertaining to overall water quality. The Clean Water Act uses both, and students should recognize the conceptual difference behind a specific rule when they see it, depending on which type it is. **Answer (B) is incorrect,** even though the definition of "technology-based" standards is fine, because the description of water-quality standards more accurately describes the "effluent limitations" imposed under the CWA than the health-based water-quality standards. **Answer (C) is incorrect** because it inverts the correct definitions for the two terms. **Answer (D) is incorrect** because the second part is tautological and inaccurate — the level of pollutants in the discharge is the "effluent" level, whereas water-quality standards pertain to the overall body of water itself.

131.   **Eutrophication** is the process by which a body of natural water has an algae bloom, and comes to resemble a green "Slushy."

132.   **Answer (B) is correct.** "Point source" is perhaps the most common phrase in Clean Water Act cases, and the quintessential example is a drainage pipe through which a facility discharges liquid waste. **Answer (A) is not the best answer,** although courts have occasionally held that collected water in troughs or ditches can be a "point source" under the CWA. **Answer (C) is incorrect;** this uses the actual words in their common meanings instead of the technical meanings given them by the CWA. **Answer (D) is incorrect;** a hill that pitches rain water toward a stream would normally be considered a "nonpoint source."

133.   **Answer (C) is the correct answer.** The classic nonpoint source is an open field, of special concern where there are agricultural uses. Rainwater picks up the chemical fertilizers, pesticides, and animal manure on the surface of agricultural fields and carries these substances into the nearby streams and rivers. **Answer (A) is incorrect;** this is a good description of a "point source" under the Clean Water Act. **Answer (B) is incorrect;** this commonsense interpretation of the words ignores their technical semantic meaning in the context of the Clean Water Act. **Answer (D) is incorrect;** while this could be a point source, toxic waste sites are mostly regulated under RCRA and CERCLA.

134.   Under the Clean Water Act Section 303(d), states are required to identify waters within their borders that fail to meet water-quality standards, or **Total Maximum Daily Load**

(TMDL). The TMDL requirements are the most effective way to address the persistent problem of nonpoint source pollution (especially from storm water runoff).

135.   **Answer (A) is the correct answer.** Sections 301 and 307(b) of the Clean Water Act regulate the municipal systems for collecting wastewater from homes, commercial buildings, and industrial facilities and transporting it to a treatment plant. **Answer (B) is incorrect** because it describes only part of the POTW system. **Answer (C) is incorrect;** nonpoint sources are usually open fields or other areas (parking lots, etc.) that result in large amounts of rain runoff; the origin of nonpoint source water is usually natural (rain), rather than human in origin. **Answer (D) is incorrect;** point sources are pipes, drainage ditches, or other localized spots of liquid discharge into the environment.

136. **Answer (C) is correct.** RCRA Section 3008(d), which is codified at 42 U.S.C. 6928(d), provides criminal penalties for anyone who *knowingly* "transports or causes to be transported any hazardous waste identified or listed under this subchapter to a facility which does not have a permit under this subchapter" or who "treats, stores, or disposes of any hazardous waste identified under this subchapter . . ." This is the environmental criminal statute that prosecutors seem to use most often. The resultant litigation often hinges on which elements have "knowingly" as a modifier — that is, whether the defendant must have had some knowledge that the material was listed as hazardous under this section, or had to know that the facility lacked a permit, etc. **Answer (A) is incorrect,** although "willfully" may be an upgrade under many criminal statutes from the mental state described as "knowingly." RCRA Sec. 3008(d)'s place at the epicenter of environmental criminal enforcement has focused the attention of courts on "knowingly" instead. **Answer (B) is incorrect,** although many students may be tricked by this type of answer on a final exam. "Pollute" may seem like a logical term to use in environmental criminal statutes, but the drafters favored verbiage that focused on the everyday *actions* that caused the pollution ("transport," "dispose," etc.). **Answer (D) is incorrect,** although this term does come up frequently in other areas of environmental litigation, as most cases could have state or federal laws that are equally applicable. It can also feature prominently as part of the definition of a "responsible corporate officer."

137. **Answer (A) is correct.** This does not merit a lengthy explanation — it is simply statutory. Some Environmental Law courses devote a unit to criminal enforcement (in which case memorizing a few of these numbers will be essential), while others ignore it completely. Students should be aware that there is an additional provision in 3008(e) for a defendant who "knows that he places another person I imminent danger of death or serious bodily injury" that provides a maximum penalty of $250,000 ($1 million for corporations) and fifteen years in prison. The question, however, asked about 3008(d). **Answer (B) is incorrect** but describes the penalties under Section 309(c) of the Clean Water Act for negligent violations, rather than the statute referenced in the question. **Answer (C) is incorrect** because the environmental criminal statutes all contain some provision for possible imprisonment. **Answer (D) is incorrect,** but this describes instead the penalty under CERCLA Sec. 103(b) for a failure to notify the National Response Center of a release of a hazardous substance.

138. **Answer (C) is correct.** A "Responsible Corporate Officer" ("RCO") is a high-level employee (manager, executive, etc.) who personally becomes the defendant in a

criminal enforcement action. Usually the legal analysis for determining who is the RCO is which manager had sufficient control and supervision to ensure that hazardous wastes were handled and discarded properly. "Willful blindness" to the environmental crimes committed by subordinates can too. *See, e.g.,* 33 U.S.C. 1319(c)(6), which says that a "person" can include "any responsible corporate officer" for purposes of criminal violations under the Clean Water Act. There is no statutory parallel for RCRA, but courts have readily found that RCO's can be a "person" for purposes of RCRA liability as well. **Answer (A) is incorrect,** although students sometimes confuse this concept from their Business Organizations class with the RCO concept in Environmental Law. Both terms refer to individual liability in place of corporate liability. "Piercing the veil," however, refers to the situation where a court reaches past the liability shield that incorporation usually provides to allow judgment creditors to reach an owner of the corporation. The RCO doctrine generally targets individual managers (who might otherwise have escaped liability under the traditional *respondeat superior* doctrine), although some of these managers are also owners. **Answer (B) is incorrect,** although also an analogous concept some students might confuse with the RCO doctrine. Vicarious liability is defined as "Liability that a supervisory party (such as an employer) bears for the actionable conduct of a subordinate or associate (such as an employee) based on the relationship between the two parties." (See Black's Law Dictionary, 8th Ed.). Students should distinguish "vicarious liability" from RCO liability, even in cases where the RCO is charged with "willful blindness" to the criminal acts of subordinate employees, because the RCO has some direct connection to the malfeasance (awareness, control, etc.), unlike vicarious liability, which is based entirely on the relationship of the tortfeasor to the manager. This phrase could also be used for liabilities that parents incur for the misdeeds of their minor children, and similar relationships of authority. **Answer (D) is also incorrect;** this is basically synonymous with "vicarious liability" in the employment or business context. RCRA enforcement against individuals seeks to connect the individual with the violations described in 3008(d), rather than imputing responsibility for another's actions based solely on a legal relationship between the parties.

139. **Yes,** "generators" have ongoing liability under RCRA for contamination from hazardous wastes sent off-site. It is possible that the transporter will fail to deliver the waste to a licensed TSDF, or that the waste will be improperly handled there.

140. A solid waste can be classified as "hazardous" under RCRA either because it is a "listed" waste or because it exhibits any of the hazardous "characteristics." A "listed waste" is any substance included on the EPA's official list of hazardous wastes (there are hundreds). A "characteristic waste" is a substance that escaped inclusion on the EPA's list, but which nevertheless exhibits one of the four qualifying characteristics.

141. **Answer (D) is the correct answer.** If a substance is "listed," there is really no argument. The EPA has discretion to list substances as "hazardous waste" under the statute, and the other criteria for non-listed wastes are then irrelevant. Of course, the company might be

able to find some technical violation of the APA's Notice-and-Comment requirements to furnish the basis for a court challenge, but that was not listed as one of the options here — and it would probably merely delay the inevitable. **Answer (A) is incorrect** because the EPA has very strong enforcement powers under RCRA — it could obtain a court injunction ordering the company to stop, it could seek civil penalties, and it could prosecute the company or its managers for criminal violations. **Answer (B) is incorrect** because it is clear that the EPA has the necessary statutory authority to list substances as "hazardous." **Answer (C) is incorrect** because these four "characteristics" apply *only* to non-listed substances. Once a substance is "listed," the "characteristic" question becomes moot.

142. **Answer (C) is the correct answer.** Under the "mixture" or rule, mixtures containing a "listed" waste and a non-hazardous substance are still classified as "hazardous," even if the mixture itself is so diluted as to exhibit no hazardous characteristics. (*See* 40 C.F.R. 261.3(a)(2)(iv)). Without this rule, polluters would simply dilute their listed wastes with sand or other inert material to avoid the regulatory requirements, allowing the hazardous materials to leech out of the mixture over time after it is dumped. **Answer (A) is incorrect,** but this would be correct if the original hazardous substance were a "characteristic" waste. The question mentions a "listed" waste, so it is irrelevant whether the mixture exhibits any of the four "characteristics." **Answer (B) is also incorrect** because there is no such exemption or exclusion. RCRA does contain a list of statutory exclusions at 40 C.F.R. 261.4(b), but sand and cement are not present. **Answer (D) is incorrect** because giving away hazardous material does not shield a party from liability as a "generator." Otherwise, every generator would find some friendly recipient to take the material off their hands, with no benefit to the environment.

143. **Answer (B) is the correct answer.** Under 40 C.F.R. 261.3(a)(2)(iii), mixtures of "characteristic waste" with non-hazardous wastes escape the classification of "hazardous" as long as the mixture itself does not exhibit any of the four "characteristics" (ignitability, corrosiveness, reactivity, and toxicity). **Answer (A) is incorrect,** even though this may be true in some cases, and there may be *other* federal laws that would apply to the sale of such sludge to our country's enemies. RCRA does not address this. **Answer (C) is incorrect.** As previously discussed, the method of disposal — dumping, selling, or giving it away for free — does not matter for generator liability. **Answer (D) is incorrect,** because under RCRA, only mixtures of "listed" wastes would still be considered hazardous under these circumstances.

144. **Answer (A) is correct.** The "contained-in rule" under RCRA means that a substance can be hazardous even if it merely contains another hazardous substance in diluted form. Spilling hazardous waste in media such as soil, sediment, surface water, or ground water converts the media itself into hazardous waste under the rule. One example of the contained-in rule is 40 C.F.R. 268.2(h), regulated "hazardous debris." **Answer (B) is incorrect,** because the "derived-from" rule applies to residual compounds after the incineration or other treatment of hazardous wastes. *See* 40 C.F.R 261.3(c). In these

facts, the water starts out contaminated, without any further processing. The "derived-from" rule more often applies to ash and similar residual matter. **Answer (C) is incorrect,** because there is no such rule under RCRA — but students should watch out for garbled versions of valid RCRA rules as false answers on their exams. **Answer (D) is incorrect,** because the *Chevron* Rule is merely another terms for the *Chevron* Doctrine, which says that courts should defer to agency interpretations of ambiguities in their governing statutes.

145.   **Answer (C) is correct.** Companies often try to avoid the costly compliance with RCRA's disposal requirements by recycling and re-using the hazardous waste in some other process. While the outcome of such cases depends heavily on the specific facts involved, as a general matter the EPA contends that it has authority to regulate recycled materials like this. **Answer (A) is incorrect,** although the corporations are often unpleasantly surprised to learn that the EPA is not satisfied with their token "recycling" efforts. **Answer (B) is incorrect,** because in some cases, courts have indeed held that the EPA had authority to regulate recycled materials like this. **Answer (D) is incorrect,** because RCRA's "cradle-to-grave" approach to hazardous waste regulation means that sufficient reporting and disclosure requirements are in place that hiding such activity from the EPA would be difficult to sustain indefinitely.

146.   **Answer (C) is correct.** A "manifest" is the document (often a few pages in length) that must accompany shipments of hazardous wastes. (*See* 40 C.F.R. 262.20(a)). The EPA has an official form for manifests that it included in these regulations, EPA Form 8700-22, available 40 C.F.R. 262.App. It is usually a critical piece of evidence (i.e., almost always one of the exhibits) in RCRA litigation. **Answer (A) is incorrect,** although some institutions use terms like "manifest" in conjunction with their inspirational rhetoric. **Answer (B) is incorrect.** Although the company may have extensive reporting requirements about its production of hazardous wastes, these reports are not called the "manifest." **Answer (D) is incorrect,** although most companies will have such a plan and will submit it to the EPA as part of their permit applications, etc. The "manifest" is a shipping document.

147.   **Answer (D) is the best answer.** RCRA has strict permitting requirements for TSDF's, generally found in RCRA Sec. 3005 and 40 C.F.R. 264. **Answer (A) is incorrect,** because even though RCRA has hazardous waste exclusions for household materials, using one's land as a private landfill clearly subjects the owner to regulation and enforcement under RCRA. **Answer (B) is incorrect** because RCRA itself does not contain provisions encouraging municipal eminent domain actions. **Answer (C) is incorrect,** although this is the second-best answer, because it is partly right. The EPA would indeed classify this as a TSDF and require "manifests" for shipments received, but this falls short of being a complete answer like Answer (D).

148.   **Answer (B) is the correct answer.** If a substance is not a "listed waste," it can still qualify as a "hazardous waste" under RCRA if it has one of these four

characteristics: *toxicity, corrosiveness, ignitability, and reactivity.* (*See* 40 C.F.R. 261.20). If the substance exhibits any of these four characteristics, it is a "hazardous" waste. The regulations provide explicit definitions for each of these four characteristics in 40 C.F.R. 261.21-261.24. **Answer (A) is incorrect,** because "lethality" is not one of the four characteristics (this seems to be an approximate synonym for "toxicity"), and "flammability" is not exactly the same as "ignitability." Reactivity is missing from Answer (A). **Answer (C) is also incorrect,** because it is missing "corrosiveness," and mistakenly includes "flammability." **Answer (D) is incorrect** because acidity is not one of the four characteristics (extreme acidity might be a subset of "corrosiveness"), and the list is missing "ignitability." Students should expect to memorize the four characteristics for their exams.

149. **Answer (C) is the correct answer.** The entrepreneur in this case may have other environmental statutes to worry about (obtaining CWA and TSCA permits and licenses, for example), but under RCRA, his initial obligation is merely obtaining an ID number from the EPA, scrupulously complying with the "manifest" requirements for shipments of waste, and disposing of the waste within three months. **Answer (A) is incorrect** because there is no permitting program under RCRA for generators of hazardous waste, although many generators face such requirements under other environmental statutes. In addition, the length of time for storing his wastes is incorrect. **Answer (B) is incorrect** because there is no "permit requirement" as such, although he must diligently prepare manifests and keep records of them. **Answer (D) is incorrect,** even though it has all the elements of the correct answer, because it adds a false requirement, the permit.

150. **Answer (B) is correct.** Unlike the "generator" discussed in the previous question, a "transporter" must obtain a permit from the EPA, in addition to the manifest requirement and the TSDF-disposal requirement. **Answer (A) is incorrect** because it wrongly substitutes the ID requirement for the transporter permit requirement. **Answer (C) is incorrect,** because it wrongly includes the ID requirement along with a permit requirement for transporters. For transporters, the permit will automatically assign them with the necessary identification for the EPA's purposes. **Answer (D) is incorrect,** because it substitutes the ID requirement for the transporter permit requirement, and because it wrongly substitutes "government disposal site" for "TSDF," which could be privately owned and operated.

151. **Yes, sludge is "solid waste" for purposes of RCRA.** RCRA's definitions section at 1003(27) provides that "The term 'solid waste' means any garbage, refuse, sludge from a waste treatment plant . . . and other discarded material, including solid, liquid, semisolid, or contained gaseous material . . ."

152. **Answer (A) is correct.** RCRA specifically exempts or excludes many nuclear and radioactive wastes because there are other statutes and regulations that cover these substances thoroughly. **Answer (B) is incorrect;** because such solvents are perhaps the classic example of RCRA hazardous wastes. **Answer (C) is incorrect,** because under

either the "mixture rule" (for diluted wastes, as when a polluter stirs inert sand into the sludge), or the "contained-in rule" (if the sand was naturally on the ground, and the waste leeched into it merely by being dumped on the ground), the resulting material is hazardous waste if the original contaminant was a "listed" waste. **Answer (D) is incorrect,** because under the "contained-in rule," contaminated groundwater can be considered hazardous waste by the EPA.

153. **Answer (C) is correct.** Fortunately for most homeowners, there is a RCRA exclusion or exemption for "household wastes" found at 40 C.F.R. 261.4(b). **Answer (A) is incorrect,** although this describes maximum penalties under RCRA 3008(d) for "knowing" violations of the statute — without the household-use exemption, this might be an accurate answer. **Answer (B) is incorrect;** first, because there is an RCRA exclusion for household wastes like those descried in these facts, and second, because the "contained-in rule" usually describes natural media (soil, groundwater, and the like) that have been contaminated with hazardous substances, and are therefore deemed hazardous themselves. **Answer (D) is incorrect** because of the household waste exclusion; even if she were a commercial establishment (in which case she might indeed be a "generator" for purposes of RCRA), she would not need to get a permit, but rather an EPA ID number.

154. **Answer (A) is correct.** RCRA is often called "cradle-to-grace" because it manages waste from the moment it is generated (by the "generator," through its transport to a disposal facility, and its final repose in a location where it will not harm the environment. **Answer (B) is incorrect,** although this is a common phrase for risk management in environmental law (especially international environmental law), describing an approach of mandatory caution or avoidance of pollution in areas of scientific uncertainty about the scope or nature of the potential injury to the environment. **Answer (C) is incorrect,** because the *Chevron* rule is a canon of judicial interpretation, whereby the judiciary defers to administrative agency interpretations of ambiguous terms in their relevant governing statutes. **Answer (D) is also incorrect;** this refers to the main approach to water pollution control under the Clean Water Act.

155. **Answer (D) is correct.** F wastes are hazardous wastes derived from sources such as spent solvents, metal baths, wastewater from industrial processes, and leachate from landfills containing one or more hazardous wastes. The CFR has a detailed table with numerous subcategories of F wastes, assigning each an industry number, an EPA waste number, and a "hazard code." (40 C.F.R Sec. 261.31). K wastes are normally generated from wood preserving, organic and inorganic chemical manufacturing, pesticide manufacturing, explosives manufacturing, petroleum manufacturing, primary metals, pharmaceutical, ink formulation, and coking processes. The CFR also breaks K wastes into subcategories. (40 C.F.R 261.32). U&P wastes include discarded commercial chemical products. P wastes are acutely hazardous wastes, and U wastes are toxic hazardous wastes. **Answer (A) is incorrect;** all of these states of hazardous waste can be considered "solid waste" under RCRA's inclusive definition of the term. **Answer (B)**

is incorrect, because this refers to three of the "characteristic" hazardous wastes (as opposed to listed hazardous wastes) under RCRA. This is probably the second-best answer, however, because the listed wastes are, in fact, categorized partly in terms of these characteristics, along with reactivity. **Answer (C) is incorrect.** Although the "listed" wastes have letter names, X-Y-Z is not the correct moniker used.

156.   **Answer (A) is correct.** Sodium metal is one example — contact with water can cause an explosive reaction. **Answer (B) is incorrect,** although this is the second best answer. Reactivity can include formation of plumes of poisonous gases upon contact with everyday liquids, but not formation of poisonous liquids. This more aptly describes "toxicity," one of the other "characteristics." **Answer (C) is incorrect,** because this really describes "corrosiveness" rather than "reactivity," even though corrosion is, in fact, a type of chemical reaction. **Answer (D) is incorrect,** because this more properly describes "ignitibility" instead of "reactivity," — even though combustion is technically a "reaction" as well.

157.   **Answer (B) is correct.** "Corrosiveness" (also called "corrosivity" in some books) refers to the characteristic of eating through (or rusting through) containers, especially metal containers, which normally hold the wastes. This allows the wastes to leak into the environment. **Answer (A) is incorrect,** although this does describe a mild type of corrosion. The EPA is focused on much more serious types of corrosion, like substances that cause holes to form in metal containers that store hazardous wastes in the ground. **Answer (C) is incorrect** because it is a misuse of the term to speak of water as "corroded." Water may be contaminated by toxic substances, but not "corroded" — although the water *could* become contaminated with a corrosive agent to the point where the water itself causes corrosion to other solids, such as metal. **Answer (D) is incorrect;** while mold and fungus may present health problems in the human environment, they are natural organisms, not "corrosion," like rust would be.

158.   **Answer (C) is correct.** RCRA's defines "solid waste'" as "any garbage, refuse . . . and other discarded material, including solid, liquid, semisolid, or contained gaseous material . . ." (*See* RCRA 1003(27)). **Answer (A) is incorrect,** even though it points to the right result, because the reasoning is wrong. The EPA would not focus on the fact that the containers are solids, because the gas inside constitutes "solid waste" under RCRA. **Answer (B) is incorrect,** because RCRA explicitly includes contained gases in its definition of "solid wastes." **Answer (D) is incorrect**; while it is true that many compressed cases are actually solids or liquids while under pressure, the definition under RCRA does not require that gases be compressed to this degree, so this point is not relevant to the analysis.

159.   **Answer (B) is correct.** The land ban has very strict requirements, including the treatment of water with the "Best Demonstrated Available Technology" (BDAT). A statute requiring BDAT ignores considerations of cost or economic feasibility. **Answer (A) is incorrect;** even though RCRA has many restrictions on the disposal of

"listed" hazardous wastes, and material containing a listed hazardous waste would itself be hazardous waste under the "mixture rule" or the "contained in rule," this is not the determination for compliance with the land ban. **Answer (C) is incorrect.** Reactivity is a characteristic for classifying hazardous wastes, but is not determinative in a land ban question. **Answer (D) is incorrect,** because this describes a lower standard than "BDAT."

160. **Answer (D) is correct.** CERCLA contains exemptions for gasoline and petroleum products, as they are already heavily regulated under a number of other statutes. **Answer (A) is incorrect,** because even if there is a release, it does not trigger CERCLA liability if the substance is specifically exempted in the CERCLA statute. **Answer (B) is incorrect;** even though the liability conclusion is correct, the reasoning is wrong — CERCLA liability does not require contamination of the water supply. **Answer (C) is incorrect;** even though CERCLA does have strict liability for potentially responsible parties, the substance here is covered by a statutory exemption.

161. **Answer (C) is correct.** Whereas some federal environmental statutes have obviated or even preempted the related common law actions, CERCLA has actually boosted associated personal injury claims because of the rich documentation the cases provide about all the possible defendants and their contribution to the contaminations. **Answer (A) is incorrect,** because unlike some federal statutes (especially the CWA), CERCLA does not preempt the related personal injury actions under state law. **Answer (B) is incorrect** because there has been a positive effect (increase) that scholars and commentators like to discuss. **Answer (D) is incorrect** because CERCLA does not have the type of disparate impact described here; many associated private causes of action would meet the requirements for federal diversity jurisdiction, given the numerous defendants and high stakes.

162. **Answer (A) is correct.** CERCLA has an "acts of God" exemption in the statute, at CERCLA Sec. 107(b), codified at 42 U.S.C. 9607(b). **Answer (B) is incorrect** because there is no CERCLA exemption for "necessary" or "useful" products per se. **Answer (C) is incorrect** because CERCLA's strict liability provisions make foreseeability irrelevant. **Answer (D) is incorrect** because there is no statutory exemption for lawyers or law firms under CERCLA.

163. **Answer (D) is correct.** There is no CERCLA liability for consumers, even if consumers are in possession of the toxic chemicals or are the reason the generator originally produced the chemicals. **Answers (A), (B), and (C) are all incorrect** for the same reason — each of these groups has statutory liability under CERCLA.

164. **Answer (B) is correct.** There is an important "lenders' exemption" under CERCLA, although it comes with certain conditions. **Answer (A) is incorrect,** CERCLA liability is not limited to generators, but can also apply to owners, arrangers, and transporters. As holder of a mortgage, one can argue that the bank had an ownership interest in the property. Without a statutory exemption (which was important lest the mortgage market

dwindle). **Answer (C) is incorrect,** although the statement is generally true, because there are certain exceptions for lenders and innocent landowners. **Answer (D) is incorrect,** because as a policy matter we do not want to discourage banks from pumping money back into the economy.

165. **Answer (C) is correct.** The lender's exception will not apply if the lender was involved enough in the control or management of the polluting enterprise to have prevented the dumping. (One could call this an exception to the lender's exception, but it is really just another way of stating the conditions of eligibility for the "innocent lender" exception.) **Answer (A) is incorrect,** because CERCLA, at least as amended, does create a few statutory exceptions. **Answer (B) is incorrect,** because the facts described here (which are not terribly unusual in the business world) would disqualify a lender for the "innocent lender" exception. **Answer (D) is incorrect,** because in the facts described here, the bank apparently could have inquired about the borrower's disposal practices and could have required that the borrower comply fully with environmental regulations.

166. **Answer (B) is the correct answer.** Municipalities get involved with contaminated sites because they operate/own municipal landfills, and they take possession of contaminated, abandoned sites through tax foreclosure. **Answer (A) is incorrect** because CERCLA litigation is abundant, yet no court has found it to be unconstitutional, despite its fearsome implications. **Answer (C) is incorrect,** although family farmland can become the subject of CERCLA litigation, often with unfortunate results for the family. **Answer (D) is incorrect,** although this is the second-best answer. Transporters are, in fact, often judgment-proof, because frequently it is a self-employed driver with an old truck as his primary asset. This shifts all the recovery actions to the remaining responsible parties.

167. **The Toxic Release Inventory ("TRI")** is an annual compilation of self-reported data on more than 650 different chemicals that companies discharge into the environment. Under Title III, Section 313 of the Superfund Amendment and Reauthorization Act of 1986 ("SARA," codified at 42 U.S.C. Sec. 11001-11050), companies must report releases of toxic chemicals to the EPA. The public can view current TRI data on the EPA's TRI website, *www.epa.gov/tri*.

168. **Answer (B) is correct.** The National Priorities List (NPL) delineates some of the most notoriously contaminated sites in the country, which are designated as recipients of federal cleanup money (which the EPA can seek to recover later fro the responsible parties). **Answer (A) is incorrect,** although such a list might be a good idea. The EPA first identifies the contaminated sites, and later looks for the potentially responsible parties (PRP's). Many of the responsible parties will not longer be in existence (corporations dissolved or bankrupt, individuals have died or disappeared, etc.). **Answer (C) is incorrect,** because the NPL is the exact opposite of what this describes. **Answer (D) is incorrect (the NPL is not just a list of government-owned properties),** although students should be aware that this is an issue in the background

of CERCLA liability. Municipal, state, and federal levels of government often end up in possession of land that requires costly cleanup, and which presents such high potential liability for any purchasers that the government itself cannot easily extract itself from ownership.

169.   **Answer (C) is the correct answer.** If a property is listed on the National Priorities List (NPL), there is a substantial risk that the landowner will face significant liability, but there is not automatic liability for any landowner. **Answer (A) is incorrect**, because Mr. Moron's liability is still tentative — it depends on whether the agency or some private party commences litigation. This is probably the second best answer, though, because his *potential* liability is nearly automatic. **Answer (B) is incorrect,** because merely attempting to purchase a property does not attach liability to the prospective buyer. **Answer (D) is incorrect** — this is the standard for RCRA, not CERCLA, and landowners certainly *can* be liable under CERCLA.

170.   **Answer (B) is correct.** There are thousands of sites that could present CERCLA liability, even though they are not included yet on the NPL. **Answer (A) is incorrect,** although the statement here is technically true, because his liability does not hinge on the property being listed on the National Priorities List, but rather the strict liability of CERCLA. **Answer (C) is incorrect,** both because his liability under CERCLA is not limited to properties on the NPL, but also because CERCLA is a strict liability statute and reliance or intent are immaterial. **Answer (D) is incorrect** because the Superfund is more likely to cover cleanup costs on NPL-listed properties than the many polluted properties that are not on the list.

171.   **Answer (A) is correct.** It is very difficult to qualify for the "innocent landowner" defense — ignorance of the pollution at time of purchase is not enough, because the landowner also has a list of affirmative duties that must be fulfilled in order to escape liability under this exception. **Answer (B) is incorrect,** because obliviousness or ignorance of the pollution, while one element or criterion for the innocent landowner defense, is only a small part of the requirements. **Answer (C) is incorrect,** because the old maxim "ignorance of the law is no excuse" applies to most environmental statutes as well. Ignorance of the law cannot shield one from CERCLA liability. **Answer (D) is incorrect,** because the innocent landowner defense does not require the landowner to do a complete cleanup (in which case it would not be much of defense), but rather to mitigate the damage as much as is reasonable (for example, try to stop ongoing discharges, seepage, or spreading of the harm).

172.   **Answer (A) is correct.** CERCLA is almost entirely focused on sites that have existing contamination, while RCRA prohibits new discharges of pollutants into the environment. **Answer (B) is incorrect,** as it is the opposite of the facts stated in the foregoing explanation — CERCLA deals with pollution that happened in the past, and RCRA forbids pollution henceforth. **Answer (C) is incorrect,** because CERCLA is not prospective, and RCRA is mostly prospective; although one could argue that is has some

"retrospective" features in that it allows after-the-fact punishments for violators of the act. **Answer (D) is incorrect** because CERCLA is entirely retrospective.

173. **Answer (B) is correct.** CERCLA allows private rights of actions by defendants against other polluters for contribution or reimbursement. **Answer (A) is incorrect,** because most of the environmental statutes have provisions by which the EPA can enjoin a polluter or stop its operations if necessary. **Answer (C) is incorrect** because apologies, however much victims like them, are not part of any federal environmental statute. **Answer (D) is incorrect** because, like **Answer (A)**, most environmental statutes give the EPA power to order a polluter to cease pollution or to cleanup a spill.

174. **Answer (C) is correct.** CERCLA covers virtually all the pollutants regulated in other environmental statutes, plus anything else that is harmful to the environment. **Answer (A) is incorrect** because the CAA regulates only airborne pollutants. **Answer (B) is incorrect** because the CWA regulated only pollutants that contaminate water. **Answer (D) is incorrect,** although this is the second-best Answer because RCRA regulates hundreds of toxic pollutants — but is still a subset of those covered by CERCLA.

175. **Answer (D) is correct.** Another distinguishing feature of CERCLA, compared to other environmental statutes, is that it focuses on contaminated *places or sites* instead of regulating particular toxins or pollutants. **Answer (A) is incorrect** — the Endangered Species Act focuses on protecting wildlife, as does, in an indirect way, NEPA. **Answer (B) is incorrect** because this more appropriately describes NEPA instead of CERCLA. **Answer (C) is incorrect** because CERCLA generally does not apply to nuclear waste materials, which are regulated under other statutes governing nuclear power and weapons manufacturing.

176. **Answer (B) is correct.** Environmental regulations that could result in liability — especially potential liability for unknown contamination — for purchases of land will generally have the effect of lowering property values. This indirect economic effect, however, is never asserted as a justification for CERCLA. **Answer (A) is incorrect,** because this *is* a common policy justification for CERCLA — it shifts costs from victims to the parties responsible. **Answer (C) is incorrect,** because is also a good justification for the otherwise burdensome strictures of CERCLA — it forces potential polluters to internalize the costs and bear them up front, instead of society having to pay the price of contamination later. **Answer (D) is also incorrect,** because the statement is true — CERCLA's mechanism for pitting co-defendants against each other saves the EPA from a lot of costly discovery and litigation work.

177. **Answer (C) is correct.** Ignorance alone is not enough to qualify a purchaser as an "innocent landowner" for purposes of CERCLA — due diligence beforehand is required, that is, checking for contamination before purchasing the property. **Answer (A) is incorrect;** it is not excuse that someone is buying and selling properties quickly and does not have time to investigate the property. Even temporary ownership can trigger potential CERCLA liability. **Answer (B) is incorrect,** because the federal government

gives no special treatment to land speculators, regardless of the supposed beneficial effects that such special treatment might have on the real estate market. In addition, CERCLA's provisions encouraging private causes of action again fellow polluters would make any favoritism on the part of the EPA less relevant for a defendant. **Answer (D) is also incorrect,** even if the statement is partly true. Often the EPA has very few solvent PRPs to choose from, and the ones most likely to be solvent at the time of the EPA's enforcement are larger corporations with significant assets. Even though the EPA may seem to target wealthier defendants in CERCLA actions, because of the limited options for solvent defendants, this is not related to the "innocent landowner" defense at all, which was the question asked in this problem.

178. **Answer (D) is the correct answer.** Promises and letters from sellers do not immunize the purchaser against CERCLA liability; the document has no relevance for the EPA, regardless of reliance or other issues. At best, it furnishes the buyer with a contract claim against the seller. This claim (in contracts) will be subject to the standard rules about contract formation, the Statute of Frauds, and contractual damages, and may be less strategic for the buyer than bringing a CERCLA contribution action against the seller after paying the sum demanded by the EPA. **Answer (A) is incorrect,** although this is the second-best answer. The letter is legally irrelevant to CERCLA actions brought by the government, but it may be legally relevant for litigation between private parties seeking contribution or indemnification. **Answer (B) is incorrect** because private parties cannot make mutual contracts that bind a government agency that is not a party to the contract. **Answer (C) is incorrect,** because the letter and reliance upon it will have no bearing on whether the EPA brings a successful CERCLA action against Harry. Reliance may indeed be relevant for his private contract claim against the seller (for example, if there is no consideration or other essential requirements for contract formation, and Harry decides to bring a contract action under a theory of Promissory Estoppel instead). Promissory estoppel will probably prove to be a weaker case than Harry's CERCLA contribution action against the seller, so he is likely to pursue his best option as a litigation strategy instead.

179. **Answer (B) is the correct answer.** "PRP" is part of the "alphabet soup" that pervades environmental law — there are many abbreviations that simply need to be memorized in order to read and understand the cases. The "Potentially Responsible Parties" are the cast of characters in a CERCLA action, and the list is often quite long. **Answers (A), (C), and (D) are simply incorrect,** but plausible-sounding, phrases for which PRP could be the abbreviation.

180. **Answer (D) is correct.** The NPL is the list of specified sites under the NCP. **Answer (A) is incorrect,** although this may trick some students because the Superfund is the name of the reserve of money for cleaning up these designated sites. **Answer (B) is incorrect;** this appellation is used alternatively for twelve famous contaminated sites in North America (the NPL is much longer than twelve!), or for the twelve Persistent Organic Pesticides targeted by the Stockholm Convention, a more recent development in

International Environmental Law. **Answer (C) is incorrect,** but is also a term related to Superfund and CERCLA liability; "brownfields" are the abandoned, deteriorating buildings in urban centers whose potential CERCLA liability for new owners is so high that nobody wants the property, and it is left to sit idle.

181.   **The Hazard Ranking System ("HRS")** "is a scoring system used to assess the relative threat associated with actual or potential releases of hazardous substances from a site." (*See* 53 Fed. Reg. 51961-62, "Proposed Rule on Revision of the Hazard Ranking System"). The EPA determines the HRS score for a site by considering several factors, such as the toxicity of the substances there, waste quantity, nearby population, surface water quality, migration routes or "pathways," etc. The scoring system has been very controversial and the subject of intense litigation. Amendments to CERCLA required revisions of the scoring system at Subsection 105(c)(2), codified at 42 U.S.C. 9605(c)(2). A score of 28.50 means that the site will be added to the National Priorities List. The notorious Love Canal site in Niagara Falls, NY has a score of 55.28.

182.   **Answer (D) is correct,** because CERCLA was designed to reach back in time to find responsible parties who could help bear the costs of cleaning up terribly contaminated sites. **Answer (A) is incorrect,** although this is the second best answer, because the *ex post facto* clause of the U.S. Constitution can indeed be relevant to retroactive statutes, but mostly criminal statutes. CERCLA liability as described here is technically civil, not criminal, although one could argue in an essay that regulatory enforcement is always quasi-criminal. Courts apply the *ex post facto* clause to criminal statutes, and only rarely, if ever, to civil statutes. **Answer (B) is incorrect** because CERCLA is explicitly retroactive. **Answer (C) is also incorrect** because CERCLA is generally a strict liability statute, so ignorance of the potential harms is irrelevant (even though it *would* be relevant in torts to show negligence).

183.   **Answer (C) is correct** because CERCLA imposes strict liability, so ignorance of the potential harms is irrelevant (even though it *would* be relevant in torts to show negligence). **Answer (A) is incorrect,** because there is no scienter requirement for general CERCLA liability. **Answer (B) is incorrect** for the same reason — intent and purpose do not shield a potentially responsible party from CERCLA liability. **Answer (D) is incorrect** because there is no such presumption — the polluter's state of mind is simply immaterial.

184.   **Answer (A) is correct.** CERCLA's definitions are expansive and inclusive. **Answer (B) is incorrect,** because even if Grandpa Jones could find evidence showing a break in the chain of causation, the elements of CERCLA would impute liability anyway. **Answer (C) is incorrect,** but it is probably the second best answer here. Barrels of waste are far beyond the threshold of "de minimis," regardless of how small it is by comparison to other contributors. **Answer (D) is incorrect** because the migration of one contributor's toxin is irrelevant for his status as a defendant or "responsible party" under CERCLA,

although it might possibly be relevant in a private indemnification or contribution suit against other polluters.

185.   **Answer (D) is the correct answer.** Defendants who decline the EPA's settlement offer take a significant risk, because the other responsible parties essentially have immunity against future contribution suits by other defendants. The policy rationale is to encourage settlements, because litigation over CERCLA liability consumes resources that could be spent on cleanups. **Answer (A) is incorrect.** CERCLA presumes joint and several liability, so each party can face full liability for all the damage. Subsequent contribution actions seek apportionment based on relative fault or contribution, rather than dividing everything equally. **Answer (B) is incorrect,** because the other responsible parties are out of the case forever once they accept the EPA's settlement offer. **Answer (C) is incorrect,** because the courts scrupulously honor the settlements already reached by the EPA in a CERCLA suit, and impute all the remaining costs to the recalcitrant defendants.

186.   **Answer (A) is correct.** CERCLA's definition of "person" includes government entities. While the scenario here may not be very likely, it *is* very common that municipalities are potentially responsible parties in CERCLA actions. **Answer (B) is incorrect,** because government agencies are not necessarily immune from CERCLA actions. **Answer (C) is also incorrect,** because there is no statutory immunity for the CIA — although the CIA's contribution may remain undiscovered because so many of its files and activities are classified. **Answer (D) is incorrect,** because any immunity the CIA gets from CERCLA will not be based on the definition of "person."

187.   **Answer (B) is correct,** because the actions described here make Dolt a "transporter," under CERCLA. **Answer (A) is incorrect,** because "owner" liability under CERCLA refers to owners of the land (real estate) involved, not owners of the vehicles or containers involved. **Answer (C) is incorrect** because "arranger" liability usually refers to those who hire the transporter and obtain permission from the landowner to deposit the contaminants on the property. **Answer (D) is incorrect,** because the "generator" is the entity that produces the contaminants in the first place, not the one who transports them and deposits them at the site.

188.   **Answer (B) is correct.** Minor technical differences in chemicals are not enough to escape liability under CERCLA, which requires only that the chemicals found at the site are substantially the same as those deposited there by the potentially responsible party. The quantities deposited are also not relevant. **Answer (A) is incorrect,** although this is probably the second best answer here, because even very small quantities are enough to trigger CERCLA liability; the amounts described here are probably too great to constitute a "de minimis" defense. **Answer (C) is incorrect,** because small variations at the molecular level are very common, even in different batches of the product being shipped from the same facility, so liability would still apply under the statute.

Answer (D) is incorrect, because intentionality does not matter in a strict liability case, such as a CERCLA action.

189.   **Answer (D) is the best answer.** The company produces the toxin that ended up in the dump, albeit in the deposits that collected on ceiling and floor tiles. **Answer (A) is incorrect,** because "owners" under CERCLA are landowners. **Answer (B) is incorrect,** although this is the second-best answer (worth mentioning if this were an essay question); while the company here might meet the elements for an arranger under CERCLA, it is clearer (and easier for the EPA to prove) that they were generators. **Answer (C) is incorrect** because the transporter here is the subcontractor who hauled the renovation debris to the dump.

190.   **Answer (C) is correct.** CERCLA creates joint and several liability for every potentially responsible party. **Answer (A) is incorrect,** but this is the second best answer, because the defendant might reach the same result (pro-rate shares) by bringing private contribution actions against the remaining polluters. In the EPA's action, however, liability is joint and several, and there is unlikely to be perfect apportionment. **Answer (B) is incorrect,** because CERCLA is a strict liability statute and willfulness does not define liability. **Answer (D) is incorrect** because even divisions of liability are extremely unlikely in a CERCLA case like this.

191.   **Answer (C) is correct.** CERCLA gives the EPA two tools that it can use in response to hazardous waste contamination. The first is remediation, that is, compelled cleanup. This option is frequently used so that the EPA does not have to expend its own funds to remedy the contamination. Remediation allows the EPA to compel PRPs to decontaminate or remediate the site. Second is recovery of cleanup costs. Instead of forcing someone to clean up the hazardous waste release, the EPA has the option to clean up the release itself and recover the costs from Potentially Responsible Parties. **Answers (A), (B), and (D) are incorrect** because repudiation, removal, and restoration are not accurate descriptions of options that the EPA has at its disposal in responding to a hazardous waste release.

192.   **Answer (A) is correct.** Section 107 of CERCLA provides that "potentially responsible parties" (PRP's) can be liable for the cost of cleaning up hazardous waste releases. PRP's include the owner or operator of the facility at the time of release, as well as the person who arranged for disposal of the hazardous waste. PRP's are liable for, among other things, any necessary costs of response incurred by another person consistent with the National Contingency Plan (NCP). In order for a private party to recover cleanup costs under Sec. 107, their cleanup costs must be consistent with the NCP (contrast with the government's recovery, where their costs cannot be inconsistent with the NCP). The NCP are regulations that lay out the procedures that must be followed in cleaning up the hazardous waste and how extensive the cleanup must be. **Answer (B) is incorrect** because government approval is not a prerequisite to recovering cleanup costs under the NCP. **Answer (C) is incorrect** because CERCLA actions are completely governed by

the statute, not by its common-law predecessors (like nuisance). A separate nuisance action by victims of the contamination may piggy-back on the CERCLA litigation, but the EPA will not be a party in that case. **Answer (D) is incorrect** because CERCLA gives private individuals, as well as the government, the ability to recover cleanup costs.

193. **Answer (C) is correct.** In general, any current owner of a facility is liable for cleanup costs and damages. CERCLA exempts lenders (who have an ownership interest in the form of the mortgage) from this general rule, with certain conditions. A bank that owns property through a security interest is exempted from liability, as long as it does not participate in management of the facility. Lenders can escape liability even after foreclosing on the property, as long as it takes steps to sell the property. **Answer (A) is incorrect** because, as discussed, the statute now extends the exemption so that it covers most lenders even when they must foreclose on the property, which otherwise would make them an outright owner until the property is sold or auctioned. **Answer (B) is incorrect** because CERCLA does not impose this duty on lenders, unless there are facts indicating that the lender had this level of involvement with the PRP-mortgagee. **Answer (D) is incorrect,** but this is the second-best answer. Most lenders do not have enough involvement in the borrower's activities to have this knowledge or to intervene. In special cases where the lender does monitor the regular business activities, and exercises some control, the exemption may not apply.

194. **Answer (D) is correct.** Normally, anyone who knows of a release of hazardous waste must report the release. The obligation to report arises if the release is of at least one pound in a 24-hour period. CERCLA provides an affirmative defense, however, where the release was a "federally permitted release." This occurs, for example, where the release complies with an NPDES permit under the CWA. **Answer (A) is incorrect** because, as discussed, the reporting requirement is limited by certain affirmative defenses, such as the "federally permitted release." **Answer (B) is incorrect** because the facts gave no reason to suspect that the permit was issued improperly; it was not "clearly a mistake." **Answer (C) is incorrect,** because normally anyone who knows of a hazardous release has a duty to report it.

195. A "Section 106 Order" is the practitioner's term for a unilateral administrative order by the EPA to private parties (that is, PRPs) requiring them to clean up a contaminated site. Under Section 106(a) of CERCLA, the EPA can issue administrative orders or seek injunctive relief (through a federal court order) mandating a cleanup. This is often a preferable alternative to the EPA's other primary option, a "Section 104 Action," in which the EPA itself expends the funds to perform the cleanup, and seeks to recover its costs later.

196. **Answer (A) is correct.** The National Contingency Plan (NCP) governs the allocation of Superfund resources. **Answer (B) is incorrect,** because the Office of Management and Budget (OMB) does not have control over the Superfund, even if it does exert some control over the EPA's ability to promulgate new regulations under Executive Order

12,866. **Answer (C) is also incorrect,** because the Council on Environmental Quality (CEQ) promulgates regulations pertaining to NEPA, collects and reviews Environmental Impact Statements from federal agencies, and prepares a comprehensive annual report on the state of the environment in the United States. **Answer (D) is incorrect,** although most agencies, including the EPA, feel some pressure to please and appease this powerful Senate committee, which exerts significant influence over annual budgets for agencies and their projects.

197.   **Answer (A) is correct.** Rico is a RCO (Responsible Corporate Officer) because he was in a position with sufficient authority and control to have ensured that the dumping did not occur. **Answer (B) is incorrect,** because it misstates the RCO rule. The RCO doctrine holds that individual managers can be liable, and do not have the traditional liability shields of the corporate veil and *respondeat superior.* **Answer (C) is also incorrect,** although this highlights the difference between the RCO doctrine and the traditional *respondeat superior* doctrine in tort law. The EPA regularly targets individual managers and officers of corporations for the environmental misdeeds the company committed under their watch. Of course, students should keep in mind that many executives have contractual indemnification agreements with their companies, so the company will have to reimburse the RCO for any judgments rendered. This contractual arrangement is not legally relevant to CERCLA or EPA enforcement. **Answer (D) is incorrect,** but it does illustrate some of the contradictions in our legal system regarding the obligations we place on managers and directors. Officers do have a fiduciary duty to their shareholders, by law, to maximize profits. This implies a corollary duty to avoid waste or unnecessary costs. Some corporate managers could therefore feel pressured to dispose of waste as cheaply as possible, especially where the risk of environmental liability seems quite remote. On the other hand, exposing the corporation to unnecessary liability could itself be a breach of the officer's fiduciary duty, and in hindsight the liability always seems more obvious and likely than it did at the time of the decision. Nevertheless, the officer's fiduciary duties to the shareholders will not be an issue in the CERCLA case — it is not relevant — even if it becomes the subject of related, but separate, litigation.

198.   **Answer (C) is correct;** CERCLA includes a remarkably expansive definition of causation compared to traditional tort law. **Answer (A) is incorrect,** because "proximate causation" is merely common-law "legal causation." While one could argue that any legal definition of causation — including CERCLA's — is therefore "proximate causation," CERCLA causation is readily distinguishable from causation in traditional tort law. **Answer (B) is also incorrect,** because this is the opposite of the actual facts — CERCLA has an inclusive definition of causation so that a maximum number of co-defendants can face liability for the same polluted site. **Answer (D) is incorrect,** although causation in these pollution cases may necessitate expert scientific testimony anyway.

199. **Answer (D) is correct.** The EPA normally tries to settle with as many defendants as possible, keeping in mind that their main goal is to clean up the environment (recovering cleanup costs furthers this goal), not to punish the PRPs. The costs of protracted CERCLA litigation are quite high and the resources could be spent instead on cleanup costs. **Answer (A) is incorrect;** even though CERCLA is a strict-liability statute, this does not prevent the government from settling with defendants. **Answers (B) and (C) are incorrect,** because the EPA can settle just as easily with individual defendants as with corporate defendants, notwithstanding the fact that individual defendants are more likely to be judgment-proof.

200.   **Answer (D) is correct.** FIFRA (The Federal Insecticide, Fungicide, and Rodenticide Act), 7 U.S.C. Sec. 136, is the primary federal statute regulating the manufacture and use of pesticide. Its main effect is to require all pesticides be registered with the EPA. Selling unregistered pesticides, under the Act, is prohibited. **Answer (A) is incorrect.** RCRA refers to the Resource Conservation and Recovery Act. This act affects the disposal of solid and hazardous wastes. Some material that the Act applies to are hazardous waste, solid wastes (i.e. landfills), undergrounds storage tanks (i.e. underground gasoline tanks beneath gas stations), and used oil. The RCRA regulates the storage, disposal, and recycling of these materials. Students should be aware, however, that many products regulated under FIFRA could contain also substances that would implicate RCRA upon disposal or discharge into the environment. **Answer (B) is incorrect** because "CWA" refers to the Clean Water Act. This act primarily addresses water pollution. Many activities are impacted by the Act, including any discharge of pollutants into streams, lakes, or oceans; some substances contained in FIFRA regulated products could trigger liability under the CWA, but only if discharged into the water environment. **Answer (C) is incorrect.** The TSCA (The Toxic Substances Control Act) addresses the manufacture of toxic chemicals. In general, it requires manufacturers of chemicals to test the product. The Act also empowers the government to order production of chemicals that present an unreasonable risk to cease. Students should note that some FIFRA-regulated products could contain chemicals that are regulated under TSCA, especially at an earlier stage in the manufacturing process.

201.   **Answer (C) is correct,** because FIFRA's definition can include anything non-human, whether plant or animal. **Answer (A) is incorrect,** because any animal *could* constitute a "pest" under FIFRA's expansive definition. Most people think of small rodents and insects as pets, but in theory, even large animals could be (and in some places, they are). **Answer (B) is incorrect** because any plant could be a pest under FIFRA's definition. **Answer (D) is incorrect** because any animal — even those commonly kept as pets — could meet the definition of "pest" under FIFRA.

202.   **Answer (B) is correct.** The primary tools that FIFRA uses to enforce its requirements are registration and labeling. The Act requires all pesticides be registered with the EPA. The sale of unregistered pesticides is prohibited. To become registered, the EPA must find that the pesticide is effective, labeling requirements have been complied with, and that the pesticide will not cause unreasonable adverse affects on the environment. **Answer (A) is incorrect** because FIFRA does not mandate that the EPA engage in negotiated rulemaking. **Answer (C) is incorrect** because, while the Act imposes some

restrictions on pesticide users, it does not require that the user be licensed. For example, the use of unregistered pesticides is prohibited. The EPA can also restrict the use of pesticides by imposing condition on its use and requiring certain labels. Users are not required, however, to be licensed to use pesticides. **Answer (D) is incorrect** because FIFRA does not impose technology-based requirements. This type of requirement appears frequently under the Clean Water Act and some other statutes. Technology-based requirements typically require that the best available technology be used to control pollution.

203.   **Answer (D) is correct.** This has actually become a serious environmental problem and the subject of the Stockholm Convention on Persistent Organic Pesticides. Many deadly pesticides remain in the environment for years (or even centuries), and the accumulated effect over time can be significant. Oil-soluble pesticides tend to migrate to the polar regions due to ocean currents and the food chain (larger animals with more body fat tend to inhabit colder climates, and their bodies accumulate higher concentrations of these toxins). **Answers (A), (B), and (C)** each describe registration requirements under FIFRA, so none of these is the best answer to this question. The question asked which of the four was *not* an element under FIFRA. The three primary requirements that must be met in order to qualify for registration are (1) that the pesticide be effective, (2) that the manufacturer complies with the labeling requirements, and (3) that the pesticide does not pose an unreasonably dangerous threat to the environment/humans.

204.   **Answer (B) is correct.** The EPA has the power to cancel or suspend the use of a pesticide if it finds that continued use of the pesticide would cause unreasonable harm to the environment. A suspension is the more drastic of the two administrative orders because if it is granted, it requires immediate cessation of all uses of the pesticide. On the other hand, a cancellation will likely not result in immediate cessation. Cancellation proceedings typically last for an extended period of time, and the pesticide can be used during that time. In some circumstances, the use of a pesticide can be suspended pending cancellation proceedings. **Answer (A) is incorrect** because, although it is true that cancellation of a pesticide could be permanent, the immediate cessation required by a suspension order is probably more drastic. Financially, it is probably more injurious to the manufacturer; retailers find themselves with unsold stockpiles of the product that are suddenly unmarketable; and consumers who want to comply with the order (like large franchise exterminators, etc.) will need to buy supplies from competitors to the firm whose product was suspended. **Answer (C) is incorrect** because, as discussed, the difference in effect of a suspension as compared to a cancellation is drastic, particularly the time at which the use of the pesticide must cease. **Answer (D) is incorrect** because FIFRA does not mandate that fines be imposed on the manufacturer of a cancelled pesticide. The economic harm may be sufficient.

205.   **Answer (C) is correct.** The inclusion of the "reasonableness" requirement mandates a cost-benefit analysis. The determination requires consideration of any benefits the activity generates compared to the possible harms that can result. Under this statute, it

is possible that a pesticide is so beneficial (such as anti-mosquito sprays that reduce mosquito-borne diseases) as to offset its small risk to humans. If the agency finds sufficient benefits from the pesticide, it might find that a small risk of harm is not unreasonable. **Answer (A) is incorrect.** Including "reasonability" necessarily means that FIFRA and TSCA do not carry strict liability. A strict liability offense does not include a consideration of whether the activity was reasonable. **Answer (B) is incorrect,** although this is probably the second-best answer here. Negligence standards like the "duty of care" do indeed involve some policy judgments and weighing of different factors, but the "reasonableness" criteria under these environmental statutes is a much more explicit cost-benefit analysis. **Answer (D) is also incorrect,** because "reasonableness" does not necessarily reflect a zero tolerance for carcinogens. At least 500 substances can cause cancer in sufficient quantities, but sometimes the risk is quite low.

206. **Answer (A) is correct.** There is no citizen-suit provision under FIFRA, unlike most environmental statutes. Enforcement of the Act lies with the EPA through its registration and labeling requirements. **Answer (B) is incorrect** because agricultural uses are not exempt; in fact, this is the primary use of pesticides. **Answer (C) is incorrect** for two reasons. First, even if Farmer Thoreau's claim has some merit, the Act must authorize him to sue through a citizen-suit provision, and it does not. Second, the "reasonability" requirement in FIFRA applies to the risk of harm the pesticide poses in the environment, not necessarily the reasonableness of its use. **Answer (D) is incorrect** because FIFRA does not protect property rights of individuals from interference by others. The Act's primary effect is to require registration and labeling.

207. **Answer (A) is correct.** Under FIFRA, use of a pesticide can continue pending cancellation proceedings. The EPA can, however, issue a suspension order if it finds that the pesticide poses an imminent hazard. **Answer (B) is incorrect** because these proceedings under FIFRA are not an informal adjudication. **Answer (C) is incorrect** because, as discussed, a pesticide can be used pending the final cancellation order. This is different from a suspension order, which requires immediate cessation of all uses. **Answer (D) is incorrect** because FIFRA does not contain this type of provision. A single human death from a pesticide does not mean that its suspension or cancellation will automatically follow. The agency will weigh all the costs and benefits in making such decisions.

208. **Answer (B) is correct.** FIFRA contains explicit preemption provisions: "states shall not impose or continue in effect any requirements for labeling or packaging in addition to or different from those required." (*See* 21 U.S.C. 136v(b)). The United States Supreme Court recently reviewed the preemption provision of this statute, and held that state courts cannot require warnings on pesticide labels beyond what the EPA has already required. *See Bates v. Dow Agrosciences,* 544 U.S. 431 (2005). Given the facts here, FIFRA preempts state tort actions based on inadequate labeling of pesticides. The Court did allow state requirements that are "equivalent" to the EPA warnings. Even so, but specifically noted that it would be improper for a court to find liability for a manufacturer failing to

say "Danger!" instead of "Caution." (*Id.* at 453). The trial court, therefore, could not hold the manufacturer liable for failing to warn about blindness, if the label complied with the EPA's requirements. The plaintiffs might have a valid cause of action under some other tort theory, like defective product design, but not based on the label itself. **Answer (A) is incorrect,** even though most pesticides are indeed inherently dangerous. The facts here ask whether the plaintiffs can base their claim on the label alone, which presents a preemption problem. The court would dismiss the case due to preemption without reaching the merits. If the plaintiffs had indeed based their claim on defective product design, negligent manufacture, etc. there would be no preemption problem under FIFRA. Of course, but these types of actions present special evidentiary obstacles for plaintiffs, so many plaintiffs' lawyers prefer to sue for inadequate labeling when possible. **Answer (C) is incorrect,** because FIFRA has no such provisions. **Answer (D) is incorrect** for two reasons. First, the preemption issue would keep a court from reaching the merits of the case. Second, if the court did reach the merits, this phrase is probably too vague to shield the manufacturer from liability for an injury as serious as permanent blindness.

209.   **Answer (D) is correct.** TSCA applies to all chemicals and mixtures, but exempts pesticides, food additives, and narcotics. The Act specifically applies to polychlorinated biphenyls, or PCBs. **Answers (A), (B), and (C) are incorrect** because they each reflect substances that are excluded from the TSCA, regardless of their toxicity.

210.   **Answer (C) is correct.** Section 4 of TSCA permits the EPA to require testing of new substances to determine their effects on health and the environment. **Answer (A) is incorrect** because the EPA is not likely to ban the substance as a first step. Before that happens, the EPA will probably require some testing and submission of research data. **Answer (B) is incorrect,** first because the question asks about TSCA applications, not CERCLA, and secondly because CERCLA would only apply if the substance were toxic and was dumped or discharged into the environment. The EPA will not identify Dr. Mork as a "PRP" unless there is a site that requires cleanup under CERCLA. **Answer (D) is incorrect** because TSCA does not give the EPA the statutory authority to seize the substance through "eminent domain." This answer may trick some students (be careful on your final exam!) because TSCA *does* give the EPA powers to sue *in rem* to seize illegally manufactured, processed, or distributed substances.

211.   **Answer (B) is correct.** TSCA Section 20 provides for citizens' suits, but does not allow for the award of monetary damages to plaintiffs. **Answer (A) is incorrect** because, as discussed, the group does have the ability to sue under Section 20 of TSCA. **Answer (C) is incorrect** because TSCA requires extensive testing of many new chemicals, before mass-production or marketing begins. The newness of a chemical does not necessarily mean there is not an impressive amount of scientific data about its potential for harming the environment. **Answer (D) is also incorrect.** This answer reflects the "injury-in-fact" requirement of standing, which is a constitutional prerequisite to bringing suit. *Lujan v. Defenders of Wildlife,* 497 U.S. 871 (1990). This question focuses on the statutory provision for citizen suits.

212.	**Answer (A) is correct.** Once Dr. Frankenstein submits (and complies) with the testing and data submission requirements, the EPA will use the information to decide whether more regulation is necessary under other provisions in TSCA. At that time, the EPA could regulate the use, labeling, and disposal of the substance. **Answer (B) is incorrect** because TSCA does not require federal agencies to prepare Environmental Impact Statements (EIS). Rather, the National Environmental Policy Act (NEPA) requires agencies to prepare these statements in certain circumstances in order to determine the effect the agency action will have on the environment. In addition, an agency does not have to prepare an EIS to determine what effect a private individual's actions will have on the environment. Finally, the EPA is generally exempt from NEPA requirements. **Answer (C) is incorrect** because there is no indication that Dr. Frankenstein's embalming chemicals will be discharged into rivers, lakes or streams. The Clean Water Act requires that if you discharge pollution into water, you must obtain an NPDES permit. Dr. Frankenstein's testing information and data is not likely to be relevant to an NPDES permit. **Answer (D) is also incorrect.** TSCA does require notice to be published in the Federal Register (*see* 15 U.S.C. 2603(d)). The required notice, however, is notice that testing data has been received. This is different from the notice required under the APA's notice-and-comment. Furthermore, TSCA Section 14 requires the EPA to keep industrial secrets confidential (production processes, etc.) when the applicant requests this, as in this case.

213.	**Answer (C) is correct.** Section 4 of the TSCA gives the EPA the power to require manufacturers to test substances in order to assess the risk of harm it poses. In addition, Section 5 requires manufacturers to do a "PMN" (pre-manufacture notification) before manufacturing a new chemical. A PMN sometimes requires more testing and data submission in addition to that submitted under Section 4. **Answer (A) is incorrect;** while the EPA clearly has authority to ban or restrict new substances (which they do in about ten percent of the cases), they do not necessarily issue permits for the production of these chemicals. **Answer (B) is incorrect** because NEPA applies only to federal agencies, not to private parties. **Answer (D) is incorrect** because, as discussed, Dr. Frankenstein must submit a PMN before he proceeds to market his new product.

214.	**Answer (C) is correct.** In addition to TSCA's testing requirements, Section 8 of the Act requires certain reporting and recordkeeping. The main effect is to require anyone who has information that a chemical substance poses a substantial risk of harm to the environment to immediately notify the EPA. There is an exemption, however, for small businesses. **Answer (A) is incorrect** because the exemption just discussed, and because there is no TSCA "whistleblower" provision. **Answer (B) is incorrect** because there is an exemption for small businesses, although this would otherwise be a good statement of the general rule. **Answer (D) is incorrect** because the EPA can use the reporting and recordkeeping requirements to learn of unknown dangers posed by chemical substances. Although the EPA might learn of most dangers from the pre-market testing and data submission, it is of course possible that such information "slips through the cracks."

215.   **Answer (B) is correct.** The TSCA includes reporting requirements. They require anyone, except for small businesses, to report to the EPA if they obtain helpful information regarding the risk of harm that a chemical substance presents. The facts indicate that Delmar works for a major petrochemical company. It is unlikely that he falls under the exemption for small businesses, so he would probably have to report the information to the EPA. **Answer (A) is incorrect** because Section 8 of the Act is not necessarily a "whistleblower" statute. **Answer (C) is incorrect** because, as discussed, the exemption in Section 8 applies to small businesses, not large conglomerate corporations. **Answer (D) is incorrect** because the EPA is not limited to the information it obtains through its testing and data submission requirements. The reporting and recordkeeping provisions empower the EPA to obtain information about a chemical substance through means other than its testing requirements.

216.   **Answer (A) is correct.** FIFRA requires that all pesticides to be registered with the EPA. To be registered by under the Act, the EPA must find that (1) the pesticide is effective, (2) the registrant has complied with certain labeling and data submission, and (3) it will not cause unreasonable adverse effects on the environment. The reasonability aspect of the third prong authorizes the EPA to consider the risk the pesticide poses in light of the economic benefits it brings. In effect, the EPA can do a cost-benefit analysis in determining a pesticide's tolerable level of risk. This mandate for cost-benefit analysis distinguishes FIFRA from some other environmental statutes. **Answer (B) is incorrect** because, as discussed, FIFRA permits the EPA to use cost-benefit analysis. This does not mandate a zero-tolerance policy. As harsh as it may seem, the fact that a pesticide presents a certain incidence of cancer in humans may be outweighed by a substantial economic benefit. **Answer (C) is incorrect** because FIFRA does not mandate a ceiling on a regulations cost. Whatever the EPA determines is reasonable, is permissible. **Answer (D) is incorrect.** The reasonability test does provide the EPA some discretion in determining what level of toxins is permissible, but the discretion is limited. The EPA must at least engage in a cost-benefit analysis and make a decision based on their findings.

217.   **Answer (D) is correct.** While it is detrimental to Discovery, and arguably unfair, the testing information and data must be public. People who register later can use the prior data, the purpose being to save money on testing. The previous registrant is not without a remedy. Under certain circumstances the EPA can require the subsequent registrants to pay the first registrant for the use of the data. In this problem, Discovery could not keep its data confidential, but might obtain compensation for Heynze if it uses Discovery's data. **Answer (A) is incorrect** because a consequence of FIFRA is that some trade secrets might be acquired by competitors. While this may be seen as an unfortunate result, the statute allows it. **Answer (B) is incorrect** because FIFRA does not contain an exception for products with "significant market potential." Even the data and testing from products that have a lot of potential are open to the public. **Answer (C) is incorrect.** Discovery might have recourse through obtaining compensation for Heynze's use of their data. Also, it would probably be very difficult to create a fungicide that could rid a salad of mushrooms.

PRACTICE FINAL EXAM: ANSWERS

218. **Answer (B) is the correct answer.** The National Environmental Policy Act requires federal agencies to prepare and submit an Environmental Impact Statement (EIS) for "major federal actions that significantly affect the quality of the human environment." The agencies must prepare and publish a Finding of No Significant Impact in the Federal Register if it intends to assert that an EIS is unwarranted for the project in question. **Answer (A) is incorrect;** even though agencies may have to prepare an "Environmental Assessment" to justify not doing an EIS, this requirement is judge-made, not from NEPA itself; it is also not clear that the EA must be published in the Federal Register. **Answer (C) is incorrect** because a Finding of No Significant Impact obviates the need for an EIS, which the agencies avoid having to do because they are so costly and time-consuming. **Answer (D) is incorrect;** while NEPA does provide for categorical exclusions of certain activities, these do not necessarily have to be prepared and published in the Federal Register.

219. **Answer (B) is the correct answer.** The attack that is most likely to prevail under these facts is the agency's failure to comply with the Notice-and-Comment requirements of the Administrative Procedures Act. The facts indicate that the agency simply announced its new regulation, effective immediately. The APA requires that proposed regulations be published in the Federal Register, that an appropriate amount of time is allowed for the public to submit comments, and that the final rule must also be published, with responses to the serious comments that were received. **Answer (A) is incorrect,** because there is no statutory duty for the agency to engage in cost-benefit analysis before making a rule, and no right for aggrieved parties to challenge the rules for failure to do so. **Answer (C) is incorrect,** because BCT is a regulatory requirement placed on polluters, not an administrative law requirement placed on agencies. **Answer (D) is incorrect** because the EPA's failure to outline sanctions or hearing procedures ahead of time does not necessarily provide a basis for pre-emptive challenge or declaratory judgment in court.

220. **Answer (B) is correct;** this is the classic common law rule for nuisance, which addresses interference with use and enjoyment of property. **Answer (A) is incorrect,** because this is the subject of a trespass action, designed to protect possessory interests and the right to exclusive control of the property. **Answer (C) is incorrect,** although some commentators contend that courts should base their nuisance decisions on these factors instead of property rights. **Answer (D) is incorrect,** because normally the length

of time one owns land does not limit the property rights, especially as opposed to neighbors; otherwise, land would have no resale value. This might trick students who are thinking about the famous *Spur v. Webb* case, included in almost all Environmental Law casebooks, which discusses a rarely-applied doctrine of "coming to the nuisance." An annoying use of land that was clear and obvious before anyone else moved into the area *might* offset the plaintiffs' property rights in a nuisance action, as in that case, but this does not mean that whoever owns their land the longest is immune from nuisance liability.

221.   These are essentially the facts of *Ocean Advocates v. U.S. Army Corps of Engineers*, 402 F.3d 846 (9th Cir. 2005). In that case, the Ninth Circuit Court of Appeals held that the group satisfied constitutional and prudential requirements of standing (that is, injury-in-fact, causation, and redressibility) and that the group had organizational standing (its directors owned shoreline property, were marine biologists, group had worked for protecting the area for 20 years, etc.).

222.   **Answer (A) is correct.** The "hard look" doctrine uses an "arbitrary and capricious" standard of review, which is supposed to be very deferential, but applies it in a very scrutinizing manner, which forces agencies to bulk up the administrative record with memoranda, scientific studies, policy analysis, etc. **Answers (B) and (C) are incorrect,** because they state the wrong standards of review under the hard look doctrine. **Answer (D) is incorrect,** even though this would otherwise be an accurate statement of what the *Chevron* Doctrine addresses, because the facts here pertain to agency decisions to regulate, not to agency interpretations of an ambiguous statute.

223.   **Answer (A) is correct.** The Clean Water Act in its original form focused on emission controls at the source — the "point source" from which pollutants are discharged into the waterways. Technology-based standards focus on the emission control devices required at the discharging source. Of course, there are also features of the Clean Water Act that utilize health based regulations, like the Total Maximum Daily Load (TMDL) requirements that states must set and enforce, but the primary focus of the CWA was technology-based. **Answer (B) is incorrect,** although most law school courses spend some time on incentive-based regulations, such as the "bubble rule" and tradable pollution credits, but these are used mostly for air pollution control. **Answer (C) is incorrect;** the Clean Air Act, not he Clean Water Act, employs mostly health-based, ambient-air regulations instead of emission control requirements. **Answer (D) is incorrect** because it is not the best answer. Both the CWA and the CAA included some "technology-forcing" regulations, but under neither statute did such regulations predominate.

224.   **Answer (C) is correct,** because the Supreme Court has held repeatedly that Congress must supply agencies with "intelligible standards" when delegating authority to them. Almost anything will suffice for "intelligible standards," but the example given here is probably egregious enough to run afoul of the rule. **Answer (A) is incorrect,** as the

Commerce Clause is rarely, if ever, used to invalidate statutes; rather, it is used to justify statutes that have no other constitutional justification. **Answer (B) is incorrect;** nothing in the example given here relates to adjudication actions against individual citizens, so no due process limitations apply. **Answer (D) is incorrect,** because this is normally grounds for invalidating criminal statutes that furnished the basis for a conviction.

225. In an action for trespass, it is irrelevant that no *person* set foot on the property of the plaintiff. It is enough that there was some *physical invasion*, even by inanimate objects like golf balls.

226. **Answer (A) is the best answer.** There is no doubt, given the extreme facts stated here, that this will be a major government action having a significant effect on the environment. The Department will have to prepare an EIS. **Answer (B) is incorrect** because agencies do not have to submit an EIS to the EPA. Rather, they submit them to the CEQ. **Answer (C) is incorrect,** because given the facts here, it is clear that the agency will have to prepare an EIS, and will probably not bother with an Environmental Assessment, which is normally done to justify the refusal to complete an EIS. **Answer (D) is incorrect,** because NEPA does not require any cost-benefit analysis, although it does require the agency to consider alternatives to the proposed project, and ways to mitigate the environmental harms from the proposed project.

227. **Answer (D) is correct.** The Clean Water Act mandates that "point sources" (a locus of discharge for pollutants into navigable waters) obtain federal permits. This is called the National Pollutant Discharge Elimination System or "NPDES" program. **Answer (A) is incorrect;** a TSDF permit is for Treatment, Storage, and Disposal Facilities under RCRA. **Answer (B) is incorrect;** the National Ambient Air Quality Standards are maximum limitations for concentrations of the six criteria pollutants in the ambient air, under the CAA. **Answer (C) is incorrect;** "NSPS" refers to New Source Performance Standards under the CWA, which must be met by new sources. They apply to all pollutants.

228. **Answer (D) is correct.** Once someone has a permit or license, it becomes a "property interest" for purposes of constitutional due process analysis, at least in most cases. This means that government agencies have to furnish some minimal procedural safeguards before revoking the permit or license, such as a "fair hearing" where the individual can hear the reasons for the revocation and can offer counterevidence. The fair hearing does not have to be a full-blown trial, or comport with the normal rules of evidence and trial procedure, but it needs to provide notice of the reasons for revocation and the opportunity for the individual to testify. Please note that if a permit or license simply expires, and the agency declines to renew it, the individual may *not* have a right to a fair hearing, because issuance and renewal is usually fully discretionary with the agencies. **Answer (A) is incorrect,** because revocations of licenses and permits are a type of informal adjudication, whereas the APA Notice-and-Comment requirements apply to agency *rulemaking*. **Answer (B) is incorrect,** because the financial burden of losing

one's permit or licenses does not give one a basis for challenging the agency decision; it is assumed that all revocations could be financially devastating, and that is the purpose of such programs, to provide some incentive for compliance with the regulations. **Answer (C) is incorrect,** because even if the EPA has general discretion to revoke permits, in many cases the holder of the permit has a "property interest" in it and therefore has some due process rights, however minimal, such as the right to an informal "fair hearing." Remember that even where agencies have discretion, they must have some reason for their decisions — they cannot be arbitrary and capricious — and the fair hearing provides a forum for the agency to show that there was some basis for the decision.

229. **Answer (B) is correct.** Under the Clean Air Act (CAA), every state had to create its own environmental protection agency that would devise a State Implementation Plan — that is, a proposal for how that state intended to comply with NAAQS standards. **Answer (A) is incorrect,** because the EIS is the implementation mechanism for NEPA, not the CAA, and does not apply to state governments. **Answer (C) is incorrect,** because a Federal Implementation Plan is the CAA's alternative when the state fails to do its part under the statute. If the state fails to submit a SIP that meets the EPA's requirements, then the EPA must make a plan for that state or region instead, which is called a FIP. **Answer (D) is incorrect,** as this is the mechanism for permits under the Clean Water Act, not the CAA.

230. **Answer (D) is the best answer.** This is very similar to the *Milwaukee II* case found in most Environmental Law casebooks, and which has taken on new relevance in modern times as states try to sue other states over greenhouse gas emissions. The Supreme Court held that the nuisance action under these facts was pre-empted by the Clean Water Act, so there was no applicable federal common law. **Answer (A), (B), and (C) are incorrect,** but illustrate the problem in this type of case — whose law should apply in a contest between states? Each state is likely to argue that the other state's law would be unfavorable, and the federal common law that was once used to resolve these types of disputes was eliminated with the enactment of a statutory regime.

231. Under RCRA, a "listed waste" is a substance that is included on the EPA's official list of hazardous substances, which means a number of strict RCRA regulations apply automatically. There are, however, many hazardous substances that are not included on the EPA's list, and new ones are invented and manufactured al the time. To deal with this reality, the regulations also specify that they apply to any substance having certain characteristics: ignitibility, corrosiveness, reactivity, and toxicity. A "characteristic" waste is a substance having one or more of these traits, and it also triggers the application of RCRA regulations, particularly for storage, transport, and disposal.

232. **Answer (A) is correct.** Under the Clean Air Act (CAA), the EPA must designate certain "criteria pollutants" for regulation by the health-based standards of the NAAQS. There are six; the EPA is very averse to adding any more to the list. **Answer (B) is incorrect;**

this designation applies to hazardous solid wastes under RCRA that have one of four "characteristics," even though they are not included on the EPA's official list of hazardous substances. **Answer (C) is also incorrect;** "listed wastes" are the other type of hazardous solid waste under RCRA besides "characteristic wastes," both other which trigger strict regulations about storage, transport, and disposal. **Answer (D) is incorrect,** because non-point sources are open fields, wide roads, and parking lots that create problems with rain runoff. These problems are regulated by the Clean Water Act, not by the NAAQS provisions of the CAA.

233. **Answer (A) is correct.** Under TSCA, Gribble's duties are normally confined to testing and notification requirements. **Answer (B) is incorrect** because TSCA does not require permits, although Gribble may have to obtain permits for disposal of wastes, byproducts, and leftover materials from manufacturing under RCRA. **Answer (C) is incorrect;** a "suspension" is a penalty under FIFRA, not under TSCA. **Answer (D) is incorrect** because NPDES permits are a feature of the Clean Water Act, not TSCA; in addition, there is no indication in the facts that Gribble is discharging into waterways.

234. **Answer (C) is correct.** The Clean Air Act focused primarily on health based regulations, i.e. the National Ambient Air Quality Standards (NAAQS). The other forms of regulation were included, of course, but the overall scheme of the CAA is health-based regulation. **Answer (A) is incorrect** because technology-based regulations were included mostly at the state level, as part of the State Implementation Plans, and were done almost entirely with the goal of complying with the existing regime of health-based standards. The Clean Water Act, in contrast, focused mostly on technology-based controls. **Answer (B) is incorrect,** even though the CAA later made extensive use of incentive-based methods like the bubble rule, tradable permits, auctions for pollution rights, etc. All of these incentive programs, however, are working within or around an existing framework of health-based regulations. **Answer (D) is incorrect;** even though some aspects of the Clean Air Act were technology-forcing — especially the regulations for mobile sources (automobile emissions), these were not the primary method of regulation.

235. **Answer (D) is the correct answer.** CERCLA's definition of hazardous or toxic substances includes most of the pollutants covered by all the other environmental statutes combined. **Answers (A), (B), and (C), therefore, are only partly correct.**

236. The typical "non-point source" under the Clean Water Act (CWA) is an open field used for agricultural purposes, although one could also suggest a paved city street or parking lot. These areas contribute to pollution primarily when it rains, and the rain runoff collects contaminants from the ground surface, carrying the pollutants to the storm gullies and eventually to the waterways. In agricultural settings, these include animal fecal wastes, pesticides, and fertilizers; in urban settings, these are usually motor oil, transmission fluid, and other substances that leak from cars. Non-point sources present

unique issues for regulators because they only "pollute" when it rains, and the rain itself is not under the control of the polluters.

237.   **Answer (B) is correct;** these are the requirements for "transporters" under RCRA, and Pete would be a "transporter" given the facts described here. **Answer (A) is incorrect** because RCRA does not require transporters to obtain permits. **Answer (C) is incorrect** because there is no permit requirement for transporters, and because it is missing the "manifest" requirement, an important feature of RCRA compliance. **Answer (D) is incorrect** because wrongly includes a permit requirement, and omits the necessary TSDF requirement for the destination of Pete's pickup.

238.   **Answer (C) is correct.** Under the strict joint-and-several liability rules of CERCLA, each Potentially Responsible Party can be liable for the full costs of cleanup, at least from the EPA's standpoint. Later, the PRP can try to sue the other PRPs for contribution. **Answer (A) is obviously incorrect;** each polluter who contributed to the contamination is responsible for the costs of cleanup. **Answers (B) and (D) are also incorrect,** for the reasons stated above (each PRP is responsible for all cleanup costs), although in subsequent recovery or contribution actions against the other PRPs, the court may use some apportionment method (undoubtedly some calculation more complicated than simply dividing by the number of contributors, give that some contributed far more than others).

239.   **Answer (A) is correct.** A suspension is the more drastic of the two administrative orders because it requires immediate cessation of all uses of the pesticide. Cancellation proceedings typically last for an extended period of time, and the pesticide can be used during that time. **Answer (B) is incorrect;** cancellation normally would not involve any finds, it would just curtail the future production of the substance. **Answer (C) is incorrect,** because modifications to the substance could work around the cancellation, and it does not require the recall or cessation from use of the substance already on the market. **Answer (D) is incorrect;** the differences between cancellation and suspension were explained above.

240.   **Answer (A) is correct.** Under *Chevron*'s two-part test, a court must first decide whether the statute's verbiage is clear and unambiguous, before proceeding to the second step. If the statute is clear, and there is no ambiguity, then the court analyzes whether the agency followed the clear meaning of the statute from an objective standpoint. The "deference" of *Chevron* comes into the analysis only if the statute is ambiguous, in which case the court must defer to the agency's interpretation, assuming it is "reasonable" (and it almost always is. In other words, if the court proceeds to step two, analyzing the agency's interpretation, then the agency almost always will win. **Answer (B) is incorrect** for the reasons stated above. It is much more difficult to prove that the agency was "unreasonable" in its interpretation of admittedly ambiguous terms, than to show that the agency deviated from an objective standard that contradicts the standard being used already by the agency. **Answer (C) is incorrect,** although many

academic commentators and judges believe interpretation of the law should be the exclusive domain of the judiciary, the *Chevron* case requires courts to defer to agency interpretations as long as the words of the statute are vague. **Answer (D) is incorrect,** because the legislative history is irrelevant for a *Chevron* case. For the first prong of the test, the court analyzes whether the actual words of the statute are clear and unambiguous, regardless of the legislative history; and the second prong requires the court to defer to the agency's interpretation, assuming it is "reasonable," even if it contradicts the legislative history.

241. **Answer (D) is correct.** NEPA has no real enforcement mechanisms except the requirement that agencies complete the EIS for major federal actions that will have a significant impact on the environment. If the EIS shows that the proposed actions will have a devastating effect on the environment, it does not mean the agency cannot proceed, although there may be intense political pressure to change course. **Answer (A) is incorrect;** the CEQ has no authority over other federal agencies and no agency would need to negotiate with the CEQ. **Answer (B) is incorrect,** because there is no requirement that the CEQ publish its reactions in the Federal Register, at least under NEPA. **Answer (C) is incorrect** because the CEQ has no power to block agencies from pursuing projects after they have completed the EIS.

242. **Answer (C) is correct.** The mix-in rule under RCRA applies to exactly this type of scenario, where hazardous substances are diluted with non-hazardous materials like sand or concrete. The company will have to comply with RCRA mix-in rules to determine the proper storage, transport, and disposal requirements. **Answer (A) is incorrect,** because the "contained-in" rule normally applies to hazardous substances that have leeched into the groundwater, making the groundwater itself hazardous and subject to regulations. **Answer (B) is incorrect,** because the "derived-from" rule pertains to residues and ashes left over after the processing or incineration of hazardous substances. **Answer (D) is incorrect,** although the "characteristic waste" rules under RCRA could help define the application of the mix-in rule under thee circumstances.

243. The EPA is likely to win under these facts, because the court will apply the two-prong *Chevron* test and will probably defer to the agency. The first prong of the test is to assess whether the statute is ambiguous, and the statutory verbiage given here seems vague enough to cover almost anything the agency wants to do. As the statute is ambiguous, the court will move on to the second prong of the test, and decide whether the agency's interpretation is "reasonable," regardless of whether it is the best interpretation or the one that Congress intended. In these facts, the interpretation seems reasonable, even if it is an unexpected interpretation, so the court would defer to the agency.

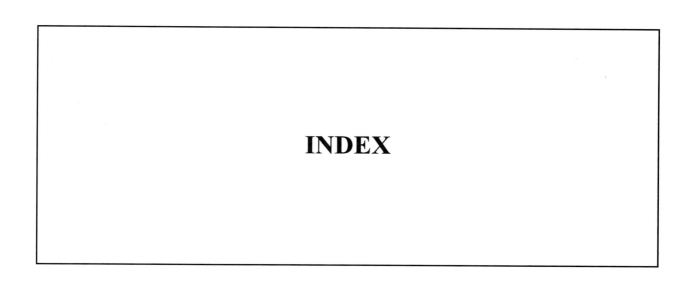

INDEX